Ebony K. English

Saved, Sober &
Sitting Pretty

Ebony K. English

ISBN: 0692064222
ISBN-13: 978-0692064221

DEDICATION

Saved, Sober & Sitting Pretty is dedicated to the memory of Monisha M. Davis and Johnny E. McCarthy, III. I could hear the cheers of my two biggest fans from the Heavenly skies throughout the entire writing process.

Ebony K. English

CONTENTS

ACKNOWLEDGMENTS

First and Foremost I would like to thank God for snatching me off the road of self-destruction, giving me the power to believe in myself and to dream again. I was desperate for change and You met me in the dark just the way I was and showed me that my pain had purpose.

My Grandmother, My Rock: Thank you for teaching me the true definition of unconditional love. I could never repay you for all the sacrifices you've made to make sure that I never went without. It is because of your prayers that I am still standing today. My only goal in life is to become someone you can be proud of and to make enough money for you to play bingo every day for the rest of your life.

My Aunts: Diane, Faye and Mini: Thank you all for always standing in the gap, so much that I literally felt my heart break the first time one of you told me, "no." I know now that it was for my greater good. I am forever grateful for everything that you all have deposited inside of me. Even when it seemed like I wasn't paying attention, I was always listening and learning. The three of you are Heaven sent and have contributed to my growth in your own unique way, but collaboratively it was the love of my aunts that saved my life.

Matt Pack: Biologically we're first cousins, in reality you're my brother! For 33 years, I have never been in your presence and felt the void of being unprotected. Although, you tortured me as a child you've never failed to display how much you love me. I know that if you had the world in the palm of your hands, you would give me half and everyone else would have to share the rest. We may be 2 deep now, but we're stronger than we have ever been...and we have an Angel watching over us. We can't lose! I hope you're ready for this climb to the top! I heard the view is better from up there.

My Jayllen (Business Manager): In raising you, I grew up! Your life is the best present that I have ever been gifted with. Everything

i

that I am is because God chose me to be your "Ma." You are forever my "why" and the reason I will never give up. Thank you for always reminding me that your mommy can do anything and pushing me daily to strive for greatness. I promise that I will never let us down.

My Mom and Dad: Thank you for the greatest gift of all, the gift of life. I am totally grateful for your blessings and support in me sharing my story.

Shuana Davis and Ebony Thomas: It was your love for God and how cool you all made your relationships with Christ seem that made me want to know more about our Savior. Because of you, I tried Jesus and it has hands down been the absolute best decision of my life. If there is anyone outside of my family that I know without a shadow of a doubt has prayed me through my mess, it is the two of you. I am blessed to have you ladies in my corner and I am striving every day to become the manifestation of your prayers.

Brandy: You have been a tremendous blessing in my life. God couldn't have chosen a better sister from another mister for me. Thank you for being a friend, travel down the road and back again. Your heart is true; you're a pal and a confidant!

MaRhonda: I made sure to capitalize the "R" lol…Thank you for being the little sister that I never had and for always reminding me to just breathe, take a deep breath and breathe again. If there was one single person that I had to thank Zeta Phi Beta for it would be you.

Sheena: I have always loved our bond, but I adore us now. It has been an amazing experience to grow from unsure girls at Benedict College to fully grown confident women and to still be able to be who we truly are in the presence of one another. You get me and I get you even when nobody else understands us that is why we will forever be a package deal. Can't have one without the other, I love you "Patty"!

Pastor Sean Dreher: I am truly thankful for your obedience and support. I appreciate the nudge.

Tameka Watson (@tamekaalicea_photography): Thank you for clicking your shutter until we captured the perfect photos for the book covers. I am forever grateful for you and I look forward to seeing your name amongst the most talented female photographers in the WORLD! I would say the sky is the limit, but your skills will take you far beyond that…I'm looking forward to crying tears of joy with you!

To my family and the countless number of friends, classmates, teachers, counselors, and co-workers who have impacted my life from Satchel Ford Elementary to Benedict College and every stage of my life in between and beyond. I sincerely appreciate and gratefully acknowledge you!

You all are forever in my heart!!

Xoxo
Ebony.

Ebony K. English

NOTE TO THE READER

Hey You,

I would personally like to extend my sincerest gratitude for your purchase of *Saved, Sober & Sitting Pretty*. Your interest in my story brings me great joy and humility as I believe there are healing powers in storytelling, which for me is a catalyst of hope and a vehicle for change. I also believe that healing begins with self-awareness, which is why without any reservations I share openly my flaws, my failures, the peaks and the pits of my life as well as the hope and strength I chased down in order to forgive and move forward. It is my pleasure to welcome you on this journey to resilience and wholeness.

I have chosen to write this book at such a time as this because people are hurting, the world is hurting and I would be extremely selfish to continue living my life with a clenched fist and someone's healing locked away in my hands.

I write especially for those of you who believe that you are damaged goods, and that your past mistakes are all that you will ever be. I want to encourage you that while you breathe, there is always hope. I pray that you end this book with the tenacity to recover and bounce back. There is no time like the present to take your power back and become the whole, confident individual that you have always dreamed of becoming.

It is my prayer that my story will sprinkle a little hope to inspire your healing where it hurts the most. I look forward to celebrating you!

With Lots of Love & Hugs
- Ebony

Ebony K. English

INTRODUCTION

In doing the inner work of becoming self- aware, I learned that I am a girl of many favorites even down to a single word. What is your favorite word isn't a first date question, neither is it one that you hear around dinner tables. Without ever being asked, people usually pick up on my favorite word pretty easily. Just as my mentor recovery coach did during one of our weekly coaching calls when she interrupted me mid-sentence to say, "It's not too often that people have a favorite word, but I think that you believe strongly in the word HOPE." "Yes, I do! It is undoubtedly my favorite word."

Hope to me is actually more than a word. It is all that I had when I didn't quite believe in myself. I hoped that one day I would. Hope is what made me lift my head off of the pillow many mornings when I was resting on defeat and wallowing in shame. Hoping to become a better person is what gave me the strength to pick up the pieces and recreate my life. It wasn't until I became hopeful that I was able to break bad habits that I hadn't previously been able to break free from. Miracles happened when I tied a knot and hung on to hope when life seemed to be unraveling around me. Hope over despair opened my eyes to endless possibilities when I struggled to see beyond my temporary circumstances.

ℬℭ

Miracles happened when I tied a knot and hung on to hope when life seemed to be unraveling around me.

Some wise person once said "we can live about forty days without food, about three days without water, about eight minutes without air, but not a single second without hope." My life is a testament to exactly what the latest version of South Carolina's license plate reads "While I breathe, I hope." Love is a beautiful word especially accompanied by genuine actions, but I was created to spread a little hope. A double shot of espresso may top the list as the world's greatest "pick me up" but turn the page and allow me to share with you how a single shot of HOPE transformed my life.

"For I know the plans I have for you, declares the Lord, plans to prosper you and not to harm you, plans to give you hope and a future." Jeremiah 29:11, NIV

1

THE STARTING POINT

Ebony K. English

Often times when I would share the result of a decision that I made with my grandmother she would say "I knew you would say that or I knew you would do it that way." I would ask her how does she always know my response before I even respond? She always smiled and said "because I know you darling! I have known you since the day you were born." A few months ago I started to explore more about that day she speak of so frequently. The day I was born, and what kind of significance did it carry for all that experienced it. For my grandmother I am her third grandchild, first granddaughter. I am also the only grandchild that shares her birth month of March. She was born on the 2nd. I was born on a Wednesday on the 7th day, in the year 1984.

Almost thirty-four years later on a good day you can still hear my grandmother referring to me as her baby. The truth is though I am the "miracle baby" of my grandmother's middle child. After three pregnancies ending in miscarriages, my mother received the dire news that she had potentially been robbed of the very essence of a woman, and told the possibility of her carrying a baby from conception to birth were zero to none. I can only imagine the shock factor of finding out she had conceived once again post an inaccurate doctor's report. At the age of 25, she carried a fourth pregnancy full term, and did the opposite of what doctors said. She gave birth to her beginning, middle and end, an only child.

I'd known since childhood that I was born out of wedlock. I was about nineteen years old when I discovered that was only partially true. I wasn't the child of the *milkman* or the *postman*, but my conception was equally as illicit. My father was wedded, my mother was not. I wasn't conceived in love; I was conceived in adultery and born a product of an affair. A society labeled "love child." As a little girl with no father in sight, with the perfect view of a mildly negligent mother, I often felt like walking evidence of a mistake.

There was a plan for my life before conception. Everything that ever happened to me was on assignment.

There was a heavy load of confusion attached to being a *miraculous illegitimate* child. My less than ideal life often forced me to question God asking why was I the child born as the result of my mother's only full term pregnancy. If God was a God of LOVE and if life was supposed to be a gift, why did my life feel more like punishment?

The answer was too complex for me to understand before I had time to mature. Just as babies have to mature in walking naturally, I had to mature in my faith walk before it would ever make sense to me that God is a lot of things, but one thing He is not is wasteful. I was basking in quiet time in my closet one morning about three years ago when He finally felt I've reached the point of maturity to where I could see the benefits of the circumstances I was born into. There was a plan for my life before conception; everything that ever happened to me was on assignment, including my parents who were casted in starring roles as pain paved the way to my promise.

2

A MOTHER'S LOVE

Ebony K. English

Did you know our most significant relationship starts from inside the womb? Our mother is our first *mirror* and she determines how we see ourselves and the fullness of who we could possibly become. My *"mirror's"* failure to consistently provide love and security returned a hazy distorted reflection of me. Unlike the little girls that grow up and strive to be like their mothers, I was nine years old when I made the decision that I wanted to be the opposite of mine.

I'd come home from school one afternoon ready to go into our apartment to eat a snack, complete my homework assignments and watch television until my mother returned home from work. Instead I got off the school bus to the sight of my yellow Charlie and the Peanuts Gang bed sheets covering all the furniture that was once in the apartment. Confused, I ran nearby to my mom's best friend house to tell her that all of our belongings were on the porch. She called my mom while she was at work to tell her what happened as she instructed me to stay with them until my mom could come get me. I didn't know at the time, but we were being evicted. The image of my sheets covering the couches on the porch instead of my twin size bed inside the apartment would be embedded in my memory forever.

My mom rushed home from work to gather our furniture and household items off the porch and made arrangements for us a place to *live*. My great grandmother generously offered us shelter at her apartment, which was located on the other side of town and required me to be transferred from Satchel Ford Elementary to J.P. Thomas Elementary. I was enrolled at John P. Thomas for two weeks before I was beat into oblivion while walking home from school one day. I remember getting up off the ground, wiping myself off and waiting for the girl to return with a stool to continue

7

beating me. I didn't think to go home until one of the other children demanded, "You better run girl." I ran all the way to home. With the little breath I had I told my mom, I hated that new school and hated those other kids more.

Either my mother was already preparing to move again or she really took heed to my emotional breakdown because a few weeks later she moved in with her new boyfriend and I moved in with my grandmother and was transferred to a third school in the fourth grade. There stood the beginning of someone lending my mom a helping hand and in return she would hand over all of her parental responsibility. I struggled to understand how separating us was the best decision. Mothers aren't supposed to walk away from their children, especially not their only child.

I adopted the false narrative that if my own mother did not love me enough to keep us together, then I must be inherently unlovable. I was vitamin "L" (love) deficient. However, the love of my aunts was supplemental and filled the gap. Aunt Diane's love was tough and kept me grounded, respectful and afraid to get out of line. She didn't spare the rod. Aunt Faye's love was playful and kept me childlike and free. Aunt Mini's love was sisterly as she is my youngest aunt. I was (still am) attached to the hip of my biological bestie. I hoarded the attention I received from my aunts and stashed it away for the moments when I needed to be reminded that I was lovable.

Most days I found comfort in my only child imagination as I envisioned the day that one of my aunts would end the running joke of my life and reveal the truth that one of them was my mother. Although I knew that was impossible because Aunt Mini is only twelve years older than me, and the other two have children the same age as me. Still yet, the most insane thoughts provided temporary sanity as I fought to piece together the disconnect that separated my mother and I. I wrestled with the thoughts of how do I make myself more lovable to my mother, when the love of everyone else came effortlessly. Why was receiving my mother's love so challenging?

The older I became, the more I missed my mother, even in her presence. I envied my friends and lived vicariously through the relationships they had with their moms. I would often catch myself staring at mothers and daughters interact in the grocery store, walking through the mall or when I would spend the night with friends. I searched long and hard for the answer to the question of why aren't me and my mother inseparable. There was no reason that made sense to an only child, especially not one of the female gender.

When I was a freshman in high school I asked myself one of the most difficult questions that needed an answer. Which one of my parents did I harbor the most resentment towards? The answer was a no-brainer, my mother. I could see my mother, physically place my hands on her, but failed to secure any healthy emotional attachments to her. For as long as I can remember I've always felt like an afterthought to her. My daddy withdrew himself from my life and didn't look back. His absence was less damaging than the unresolved resentment I had for the parent that was right in front of me.

3

DADDY'S GIRL

Ebony K. English

I'm reminded of something that I have heard my aunt say jokingly a time or two. "Your birthday is a *national holiday*; you're not supposed to do anything, except be celebrated." I took those words to heart as I made the decision to skip school on my 17th birthday, because after all, doing nothing has to include not attending school either, right? At least that's what made sense to me as I sat in my room listening to B2K (yes I was a fan) hoping and praying that my mother didn't come home and catch me taking Aunt Diane's advice on my *national holiday*. I was lying across the bed jamming to the sounds and lyrics of "Bump Bump Bump" as I heard what seemed like the sound of someone knocking on the door. I ignored the sound because I wasn't expecting anyone. My friends were still in school; my boyfriend wasn't sneaking over until after his football practice and my mom would use her key if it was her, I thought as I heard the sound again. The knocking became persistent. Nervous and afraid I was about to be caught skipping school, I tiptoed to the door to sneak a peek of whoever it was through the peephole. I noticed it was a man, but his face wasn't registering. I had never seen him before.

Having outgrown the age of following the "don't open the door for strangers" rule I did the opposite and opened the door only to lock eyes with a man I would soon find out was my daddy. "Ebony?" He asked nervously. "Yes." I answered confused. "Do you know who I am?" before I was able to answer, he continued, "I am your daddy and I know today is your special day, I wanted you to feel loved so I brought you this teddy bear and flowers to wish you a happy birthday."

We stood in the doorway, him nervous and me completely dumbfounded as an awkward silence filled the gap where neither of us had any words to speak. That moment standing outside the door captured a few firsts for me. My first real memory of my daddy and the first time I'd looked into the eyes of the man who abandoned me and whose love I was desperate for. The whole day I was worried about my mother showing up, only for my daddy to mysteriously appear after seventeen years. He never once questioned why I wasn't in school. I assumed he knew just like I did that he was not in position to be asking a lot of questions. I on the other hand needed answers. After thanking him again for the teddy bear and flowers I had to know how he found me, so I asked.

He said he had gone to C.A. Johnson High School only to be told that I was a student at Columbia High School. One of the administrators gave him our home address. Apparently one didn't have to offer much collateral back then to obtain student information. Question after question he would continue to answer, until he finally said, "I have to go." Before his departure he promised he would return to take me to dinner that evening so that we could continue our conversation. I was still perplexed, but undeniably excited at the thought that I may finally matter to my daddy. For him to show up the first time was already enough for me, but for him to be coming back for a second time in the same day was an added bonus. I went back into the apartment placed my flowers in a plastic cup filled with water, put my teddy bear on the night stand beside my bed and pressed play so that I could continue to vibe to my favorite B2K songs as I picked out an outfit to wear on my first *date* with my daddy.

As I waited up in excitement like a kid on Christmas Eve for my dad's return, the hours became longer, the clouds got darker. Tears began to form as I mustered up enough courage to call the number he had given me earlier that day. Just before I was about to hang up the phone, I heard a woman answer.

"Hello"

"Hello, may I speak to Thomas?"

"May I ask who is calling?"

"Yes ma'am this is Ebony, his *umm* daughter. I saw him today. He is supposed to come back to take me to dinner. Is everything ok?"

Nothing could have prepared me for the response that came from the voice on the other end of the phone. His mother confirmed what my gut already knew. "He's not coming back, he's tired and we don't think that you're his daughter anyway," are the only words I have ever had the pleasure of hearing my paternal grandmother speak in my life. I could feel my heart break, as the rest of my body slid down the wall. If he wasn't serious about having a relationship with me why would he show up in the first place? Not only was I not worth his time, my feelings held no value to him. Apparently, it would have been too much to ask of him to be the one to answer the phone for me that night or for him to call and tell me that he would not be returning.

Growing up I heard several stories about his family's display of hate for me as they would do malicious things such as send my mother back my baby pictures with holes poked in my face. I even *dodged a few bullets*, from his wife when she threatened to blow my brains out if she ever saw me. However, I honestly never felt like he hated me. I have always thought the only way to keep his wife quiet and his home peaceful was for him to deny me a father. My mind changed that night on my 17th birthday. He hates me too were my thoughts as I held my new white teddy bear, cried myself to sleep and accepted the fact that I just wasn't good enough for my daddy and I may never see him again.

Two years following the ultimate birthday disappointment, upon his son's release from prison, I received a phone call from one of my cousins telling me that my *brother* wanted to see me. I responded, "I don't have a brother." At that time, I was 19 years old and had always identified myself as an only child. Accepting my daddy's other two children as my siblings was no easy task and would not be placed on my "to do" list any time soon. He protected and provided for them. I was his *love child* that he didn't have any interest in loving. The three of us didn't have anything in common, but that did not stop my brother's relentless pursuit to have a relationship with me. I was very reluctant to have a simple conversation with him out of fear that most men are just like their fathers. I was too afraid that he was only going to come *tease* me, make more promises and disappear just like our daddy had done two years prior. My brother proved to be something that my daddy was not. He was consistent. To honor his consistency I decided the least I could do was accept a few of his phone calls.

I was more comfortable conversing with him over the phone than I was allowing him to visit me in person. He had just finished a prison sentence for what I understood to be a murder charge. The last problem I needed was for someone to retaliate on him while we were together. I wasn't trying to lose my life over a man I barely knew (or a man I knew well for that matter). I was adamant about not allowing him to see me until I found myself in a bind and struggling to find a ride back to campus one Sunday afternoon. Assuming those were the type of things big brothers did, I called to make a deal with him, if he was willing to give me a ride to school, I would be willing to speak to him face to face. It would be a win for all parties involved. Of course he came. He was unyielding in his plan to see me. Still very hesitant about riding with him, I loaded my clean laundry up in his car, got in and buckled my seat belt as I prayed that, that was not my final ride. I was only in his car for a few moments before he began to share some disheartening discoveries with me. His daughter lived in the apartment building directly next to the building we were living in at the time and my *sister* was working at the Arby's right up the street from the apartment complex. If that wasn't enough to break my spirit, as soon as we pulled up to the dorm he dropped his head in disbelief as he said, "Dad's house is right there on Laurel Street." Laurel Street is a less than thirty second commute from campus. My family was so close yet so far away. From that day forward, every time I rode down Laurel Street I would stare at the houses wondering which one my daddy lived in.

Two weeks later, my brother felt it was his duty as the oldest child to unite my sister and me. He called to ask if I was going to be at my mom's house that weekend so that she and I could meet. Not wanting to be caught off guard, and remembering my sister's name from a previous conversation with my brother I made a visit to Arby's to catch a glimpse of the woman with that name on her tag. It has always been my heart's desire to have an older sister, but I quickly realized as we sat in the living room of my mother's apartment on a Saturday afternoon staring at each other that her desires for a younger sister were nonexistent, especially if that little sister was the *baby* that was conceived when her daddy cheated on her mother ten years into their marriage. The words she spoke that day were proof that she'd inherited her mother's hate towards me "My daddy is not your daddy; you don't even look like us."

Outraged, I interrupted her before she could say anything else, "you can have your daddy, I don't want him just like he doesn't want me," and politely asked my brother to take his sister and get out of my mama's house. I was not in the best situation to argue with her about the father that tucked her in at night, kissed her boo boos and told her she was beautiful. She was *daddy's girl*. I was just a confused 19 year-old searching for the man that would call me his princess and tell me how beautiful and worthy I was. Enough was enough, if everybody was saying the same thing then maybe there was some truth behind it. Maybe he wasn't my daddy. There was only one way to uncover the truth, I had to face my mother. As soon as she returned home that afternoon I risked it all in asking her, "Who is my daddy?" She looked at me with disgust in her eyes and refused to respond before she went into her room and slammed the door. I did the same, before crying myself to sleep once again with no real solution to my fatherless void.

Needless to say my brother's attempt to build a relationship between my sister and I failed. However, my brother didn't allow anyone else's lack of interest in getting to know me to interrupt his desire to be in my life. We attempted to build a relationship for a few months before he found love and decided that a move to North Carolina would be ideal for new beginnings in his life. I supported his decision although the goodbye was tough to *swallow*. We didn't have enough time to bond and I knew that losing him would mean losing any possibility of having my dad in my life as well. The day before he left, he met me at the front gates of campus to say his goodbyes and to tell me that he wanted to continue cultivating our relationship. He hugged me as he kissed my forehead and asked me to stay in contact. He was certain to give me the telephone number to our daddy's home as a parting gift. I wasn't sure if that was a sentiment of love or one of spite.

His mother's hate for me was no secret. He knew the emotional damage that could be brought about if I ever decided to call their home. I wasn't in a hurry to contact my dad, so I programmed the number in my cell phone just in case I had a reason to use it in the future. Once my brother moved to North Carolina, I never spoke with him again. My fears were realized. He was exactly like our dad; all talk, no action and full of broken promises. I lost contact with the only hope I had of obtaining a relationship with my dad or anyone in his family.

I gave up on fighting the losing battle of having my daddy in my life. I may not have been conceived through ideal conditions, but that was no excuse for him to not at least try to be a decent father. Regardless of how his wife or my mother treated him because of me, giving up on your children should never be an option. I would have traded anything for a relationship with my daddy; instead, I was left to assume that I wasn't worth fighting for. In a perfect world, daddies are supposed to be the most significant man in his daughter's life, her sense of protection, an example of how every other man in the world is supposed to treat and respect her. My daddy was my greatest lesson in rejection and feelings of worthlessness. I internalized his rejection and believed that I was flawed beyond repair. Maybe I wasn't pretty enough, maybe I wasn't smart enough, maybe I didn't say the right things when he came to visit me on my 17th birthday. His rejection ultimately made me question if I would ever be good enough for anyone or anything. Often times the answer was no. If I was good enough, my daddy would have stayed and fought for me when his wife kept him from being present in my life, but he did have another daughter so there was no void for him. I didn't have another daddy though and the fatherless void set the tone for the detrimental decisions that I made in regards to my relationship with myself and the opposite sex.

ஐௐ

My daddy was my greatest lesson in rejection and feelings of worthlessness.

4

DESIRABLE

Ebony K. English

Romantic relationships were undoubtedly the area that suffered the most due to my fatherlessness. Broken and fatherless I developed a need to be accepted and loved. Dysfunctional relationships trumped not having any relationships at all. I became dangerously complacent with being mistreated and emotionally tormented as long as they didn't abandon me. My inability to keep my daddy interested in having a relationship with me caused me to challenge myself in seeing how long I could make my relationships last regardless of how unhealthy they were, beginning in my younger years.

Around the time I reached puberty it was finally paying off that my grandmother and I lived within walking distance of Sidney (Finlay) park which was Columbia's main attraction for weddings, Kid's Day, and the Summer Concert Series. One Saturday, my best friend and I were able to talk her parents into letting her come over so that we could attend May Fest, an urban festival hosted by the African American community. I didn't know what to expect from the event, but I did know that I was going to wear the one outfit that would get a lot of eyes looking in my direction. A short floral skirt set that had just enough of a cut out around the navel area to make me feel *sexy*. My friend was taller than me, with really pretty legs and long hair. I was not going to be out done.

As soon as we arrived to the park, we couldn't help but notice there were so many people, young and old, and quite honestly a very inappropriate environment for fourteen year-old girls. My best friend's dad already felt that I was a bad influence on his daughter and barely approved of our friendship. If he knew what that day would be the beginning of, she would have never gotten dropped off at my grandma's house. We were at the park for about thirty minutes before we ended up standing near a group of boys that appeared to be our age. I assume that since we were all underage and attending an event that was intended for adults is what made them notice us.

My floral outfit was working for me, catching the eye of the cutest one in the group. To me he looked a lot like the R & B singer, Ray J. He appeared to be really quiet and reserved at first. You know the guys that know they're attractive so they just stand away from the crowd licking their lips. That was him. One of the other guys asked me, "So are you gone to holla at my boy or what?" "Your boy better come holla at me." He heard my response and took the bait. We started to converse just the two of us, as my friend talked to one of his friends. The other boys just stood around seeing who else they could find in the crowd.

"What's your name?"

"Ebony"

"What's your name?"

"Wayne"

"Wayne, what?

"Dwayne"

Me: "Oh, where are you from?"

Him: "I live near Fairfield Road."

Me: "How did y'all get all the way over here? I know y'all aren't old enough to drive."

Him: "No, we got dropped off."

We flirted for a few minutes, until the other boys were ready to move along. He asked for my phone number and I told him that I couldn't have any boys call the house for me. "Man... just give me the number," he said smiling. I lost my ground and ended up giving him the number to my grandma house. "Call after 7pm, she is usually gone to play bingo around that time."

He called me that evening once they were picked up from the park and all of the other boys were gone home. We spoke every day after the May Fest. If he wanted to talk before my grandmother's *bingo hours*, he would have his sister call and ask to speak to me. Or he would call and hang up, signaling me to call him back when the coast was clear. Every Sunday for weeks, he and his friends would get dropped off at the park; I and whoever was available to walk with me would meet them there. I would push my friends, neighbors, and cousins off on his friends, while he and I were smitten for one another.

During our summer break, we turned it up a notch and started meeting at Columbia Mall and would walk to the movies once all adults were out of sight. He was always with the same boys; I was with whoever I could *use* at the time. That caused confusion as my friends and cousins started liking the same boys. None of that was any of my business though, because Dwayne was all mine and would eventually become my first boyfriend. By the end of summer vacation, it was Ebony and Wayne's world, everybody else was just visiting.

August of 1998 began our transition to high school. We were zoned for two different schools, which prompted me to beg my grandmother to enroll me at Eau Claire High School. School of choice was not an option twenty years ago, but I needed to go to school with Dwayne by any means necessary. Knowing that my favorite cousin was entering the 9th grade at Eau Claire, I suggested that maybe I could go to school from her dad's house during the week and return to my grandma's house on the weekend. My plan failed miserably and I was off to become a Columbia High Capital. I lived for the weekends so that I could see Dwayne. Things were getting pretty *serious* between the two of us. His mother even showed support of our relationship by picking me up on the weekends and taking me back to their apartment to hang out. She would monitor us, without smothering us.

Dwayne was the *perfect* boyfriend. He was good-looking, charming, humorous and most importantly he made me feel desirable. I wasn't fully aware of how he was supposed to treat me, but any young boy that would serenade his girlfriend to the tunes of Brian McKnight's, "You're the Only One for Me," had to be loving me right. About six or seven months into our relationship while lying in the bed in his room I remember him asking if I knew how to "do it." In his mind, we had already done enough *practicing*. It was time for the *real deal*. I was convinced that Dwayne was skilled in doing the "do" but I wasn't. We didn't have sex that night. He wasn't forceful. He was only guilty of planting the seed that created the thought of him *taking* my virginity. Given the right opportunity I knew that *thought* would become an actual occurrence. What I didn't know is that I

What I didn't know is that I was warming up to have my first dance with addiction.

was warming up to have my first *dance* with addiction. I was starting to crave attention from the opposite sex, specifically at that time Dwayne's. I knew that if I did not agree to have sex with him I would no longer be desirable to him. I wasn't willing to risk losing his interest in me.

I could hardly wait to get home so I could call my friend and tell her what he asked me. She asked me what was I going to do, although my mind was already made up I told her I wasn't sure. I didn't want her to try talking me out of it. When we got to school on Monday after Christmas break, I asked her if I were to lose my virginity to Dwayne would she be willing to lose her virginity to one of his friends(now I know why her dad didn't trust me). Being a bad influence on my friend didn't concern me at all. I was more worried about losing my *boyfriend*. I'd learned to prioritize the needs of the opposite sex above everything else from my mother. If I didn't "do it" someone else would have, but why would I allow that when I was his *girlfriend*? When I spoke to him that evening after school we made plans to "do it" that upcoming Saturday.

After talking my aunt into buying me a brand new black skirt to match a black and white Calvin Klein shirt I was just gifted for Christmas, I was all set for the special *occasion*. I was picked up from my grandma's house by him and one of his older friends. I smiled as I saw he was wearing one of his Christmas gifts, a blue Kansas City Royals fitted hat. I proceeded to hop in the backseat of his mother's black Rodeo SUV, and we went to Willow Run apartments. I thought that the session would take place at his house, but we ended up walking to another building where one of the other boys lived. All of his friends were there, but being around them was nothing new to me and I was sure by then that they knew the plans better than I did. He and I went into a dark room alone; not even bothering to turn the light on. I didn't have a chance to act like I didn't know what I was there for that night.

"How do we do this?" I asked as we walked over to the bed.

"Just lay down."

"Do we kiss now?" I asked nervously.

No response from him, he obliged and kissed me as he started to caress my thighs and remove my panties. I tensed up.

"Is this going to hurt?"

"I'll go slowly, it won't hurt." I trusted him.

Seconds later, I was penetrated for the first time and my

breathing paused.

"Are you ok?"

"Yes, you can keep going."

While we were getting *busy*, I heard one of his friends say my friend's name. She stuck to her word and showed up just as she promised she would. She lost her virginity that night too. Not only did we share the same birthday, but as of January 9, 1999 we had something else in common, we were no longer virgins.

We sat up on the bed once we were done and he asked me again was I ok. I told him yes I just needed a wash cloth so that I could go wipe myself off. He yelled from the room asking his friend to give me a wash cloth and told me he was going to get something to drink from out of the kitchen. Before either of us left from out of the room he told me he loved me and kissed my cheek. I went to clean myself up and then went into the kitchen. He didn't waste any time handing me a blue cup and said "drink this." It was some thick yellowish substance in the cup. I asked him what he was trying to make me drink. "It's egg yolk and vinegar, it kills sperm cells." "I'm not drinking that, you drink it." He said "I'm not the one that can get pregnant." By the time he and I were finished going back and forth, my friend was coming out of the room with a slight limp. We all laughed as Dwayne fixed her a cup of the concoction as well. Very hesitant, we both drank the egg yolk. We could hide the fact that we were now 14 years old and sexually active, but there was no way to hide being 14 years old and pregnant. Although I don't recall him *releasing* inside of me, I couldn't take any chances.

After our first sexual encounter came countless others. I had begun to equate sharing my body to being loved. If sharing my body was going to keep his attention and him 'loving' me, I was willing to have sex anytime, anywhere. Going into our junior year of high school, Dwayne became a little distant. Instead of calling every day, I may have spoken to him four times a week. Our weekend visits declined as well. I assumed since he had recently gotten a driver's license, that he was out exploring his new found freedom. He would talk to me or see me just enough to keep my emotions at bay. I like to call this the, "back pocket effect." That is when someone strays away from doing the things that has become the norm for you, but they keep you close enough to make you feel like you still matter, hence keeping you in their back pocket until they feel like taking you out, to *play* with you.

It wasn't until I received a phone call from my younger cousin that I started to realize what was happening.

"Eb, I think Dwayne has another girlfriend."

"What do you mean, he has another girlfriend?"

"I've been seeing him around school with a girl named Amanda; I think she is a senior."

My only response was to scream and hang up the phone.

When I finally gained control of my emotions, I called to ask him about the allegations my cousin presented me with. Of course he denied it and tried to make it seem as though my cousin was trying to break us up because she liked him. I didn't want to believe that he had another girlfriend; I thought I was doing everything right. He came to visit me the next day to plead his case while my mother was at work. That was one of the few times we had sex in a bed. We started in my bed and thought it would be fun to "do it" in my mother's bed too. When it was all over he went to flush the condom, but it kept getting stuck so he used a wire hanger to get it out and ended up putting it in the bathroom trashcan. I never thought to dispose of all the trash into the big dumpster outside, so while cleaning the house that following weekend my mother went to empty all of the trash from our apartment. Only to come back inside the apartment livid.

"Look what failed to make it into the big trash can?"

"What is that?" I asked.

"A used condom."

"Well, it's not mine." I said nonchalantly.

I tried to blame it on one of my friends, but she knew better. She picked up the phone and made two phone calls. The first one was to my youngest aunt. "Your niece is in here thinking she grown, having sex in my house." My aunt asked to speak to me and said, "So you having sex now?" "No, I told your sister that I don't know where that condom came from, she always making stuff up." "Whatever put Drena back on the telephone." Nothing came out of that phone call because quite frankly they were late. I'd lost my virginity two years earlier and was frequently active since the first time. It was too late to chastise me or have the "sex talk" after I'd experienced it firsthand. The second call was to Dwayne's mother. "I want you to know that Ebony and Dwayne have been having sex in my house, I found the condom they used." My mother already disliked him because of some lingering animosity towards his mother from their high school years. So any opportunity she had to break us up, she was going to take it. That was her opportunity. "He better not let me catch him at my house because I will have him arrested." That conversation didn't go over so well either, only because she threatened Dwayne. His mother already knew we were sexually active. She was probably the one that provided the condom that was found.

I wish I could say that situation made Dwayne and I stronger, but it did not. The next time I saw him he was coming to break up with me. Apparently he didn't need a girlfriend that wasn't smart enough to make sure that a condom wasn't found and I should have stopped my mother from calling his mother. The fact that we had gotten caught was all my fault and he used that as the reason for why he didn't like me anymore. He was pretty convincing, and I believed his reason to be genuine until a few days later when I was smacked with the reality of it all. As I was taking tickets at the ticket stand at AMC Dutch Square Movie Theater, when I saw the boy I loved walk up holding hands with a girl fitting the description that my cousin had given me of Amanda.

ℰℛ

My first heartbreak started the cycle of me choosing men from a wounded place.

My body responded by letting off symptoms of a *broken heart*, my knees buckled and my palms became sweaty. I eventually ended up running to the bathroom to vomit. The sight of my first love with another girl snatched the breath out of me and made me sick emotionally and physically. It was true. Dwayne had another girlfriend and showed no care or concern about my feelings. He had to pass three movie theaters before he arrived to the one I worked at. He had gone out of his way to prove he didn't *love* me anymore. He was intentional about flaunting his new relationship in my face. I felt so stupid. Everything that I thought myself to be was tied to that 17-year-old boy. Once again I was left feeling like I wasn't good enough and that my value had been depreciated due to having sex before I was mature enough to understand how emotionally traumatizing it could be. That was the first of many times I had been *dumped* in my life. My first heartbreak started the cycle of me choosing men from a wounded place. I would never leave any of my relationships no matter how emotionally compromising they were. I needed to be wanted to feel like my existence had worth.

5

LOST

Ebony K. English

In 2017, the hashtag #MeToo started trending on social media as women vulnerably shared their individual stories of sexual assault. As I witnessed the courage and strength of women across the world I was taken back to the night I was awakened by "The Tickle Monster." I vividly remember the sound of heavy breathing and the applied pressure of an extra few pounds on top of me. I thought I was trapped in a dream until I attempted to turn over and found myself unable to move. I started to wiggle, but never opened my eyes. *He* took that as a warning and carefully removed himself off of me. I squinted my eyes just enough to catch a glimpse of him on the floor crawling out of the room.

I can't honestly admit to being afraid, my first thought was not to cry out for help. My first thought was how he could possibly do that when his daughter was in the bed sleeping right next to me. That night was the beginning of my #MeToo nightmare. The next day I stared him down. It was my way of letting him know that he did not get away with his sexual perversions. Since there was no penetration, I was confused and questioned if I should tell another adult. I decided not to. It wasn't as if I was waiting to be penetrated before I said anything. I was hoping it was an isolated incident and that it would never happen again. Apparently, he wasn't appreciative of the, "forgive and forget," approach I was attempting to use because that didn't stop him from trying to force himself into my personal space.

No matter where we were, or who we were around, he would always find a way to maneuver an innocent hug into some sort of awkward embrace. It would appear to be innocent to anyone that was looking from the outside in, but it always made me uncomfortable when he would whisper, "You want to play with the tickle monster," while caressing my breast. My failure to tell anyone about the night I woke up with him on top me silently gave him permission to continue to prey on me. For years I was tight lipped about his perverted advances because I didn't want to ruin the marriage between him and my aunt, neither did I want to jeopardize the very valuable relationship that I had with her. As time progressed, he eventually stopped coming around the family as much as he once did. I'd hoped that his absence was a sign of me being safe from his inappropriate actions.

To my surprise, it wouldn't be long before another family member stepped in and picked up right where he left off. This time my personal boundaries were invaded through what could be best described as wrestling moves, he would grope my breast as well. The first couple of times were thought to be accidental. We were playful, we're cousins. There was no harm in *wrestling*. That's what I believed until one evening while I was in the living room at my grandmother's house watching a show on her floor model TV; when I was approached and put into a tight hold, while my breast were fondled once again. I knew that time was not an accident because we were not in the act of "playing".

I asked him to please leave me alone, while he said, "You better not tell anybody because I am just *playing* with you." Was he really playing or were those mind games to keep me from telling someone so that he could continue "playing" when no one was around? He'd also recently overheard a conversation between Dwayne and me so he was the only person that knew I was no longer a virgin. I was afraid he would use that against me if I told. That put me in a compromising position because I knew it would be in my favor to zip my lips about it because to tell could mean turmoil and strained relationships in my family. I wasn't prepared to carry that burden of being the person that *destroyed* the family, but I knew I wasn't in the wrong and neither would I be lying. If I didn't break the silence it could have been taken to a more traumatizing level of sexual advances. I told him if he touched me again I was going to tell my grandma. "She won't believe you, because everybody knows you're a liar." He said before proceeding to touch me again.

I yelled "STOP", broke away from him and ran upstairs to tell my grandmother. It was a matter of seconds before grandma set *hell on fire*. Within moments she was calling all of her children over to her house that night so that I could tell them what I told her. I shared everything that I experienced from my cousin and my aunt's husband. My cousin acted as if he wanted to become violent and accused me of lying, which poured salt into an open wound. My voice was silenced by all of the accusations and opinions that were *flying* across the living room, while I sat on the stairs crying and feeling like I had made a mistake by telling and protecting myself from any further sexual violations. Not everyone believed my side of the story, but the ones that did, did not hesitate to defend me. My uncle Mike did not take my cousin's threats lightly; neither did he involve himself in trying to figure out who was lying and who was not. He only wanted to protect his niece. He suggested that I come stay with him for a while, which was impossible without me having to transfer schools.

That was the night that I realized that not only did I hate men, I feared them as well. I hated the type of men like my daddy that were nowhere to be found, leaving their little girls uncovered and lacking protection in times like that when they needed them the most. I feared the type of men that would take advantage of women and young girls. I wasn't only hurting for myself that night on the stairs, I was also hurting for the daughters those two men fathered. How would they feel if someone were to violate their daughters, and then accuse them of lying? Once the arguments died down, my grandma agreed that it would be a good idea for me to go to my uncle's house for a few days. While I was upstairs packing my clothes, my grandmother looked at me with tears in her eyes and told me not to ever keep anything like that away from her again. I told her I was afraid that no one would believe me. "I will always believe you, but for now go over to Michael's house for a few days until this settles," she said as she hugged me.

ଽୢେଐ

When I left home that evening that was the last of the conversation, no one was willing to help me heal.

When I left home that evening that was the last of the conversation, no one was willing to help me heal. I just had to wear the shame and guilt and dress it up as pretty as possible. Going to stay with my uncle and his family was the best thing that could have happened once I left my grandmother's house. His home was safe and peaceful. He never took me through the torture of having to tell him my side of the story all over again. He was satisfied that he was able to protect me until the *storm* passed.

It would be a few days before I returned home to my grandma's house and school. On the morning that I returned to school my administrator called me into his office to speak with me. As I walked over to his office I was preparing to defend myself as I thought one of my teachers had written me up for consecutive absences. The look on his face was one of concern and I knew then that something more than my absences was bothering him. He asked me to sit down while he closed his office door. He looked away from me as he appeared to be fighting back tears.

"I know I cannot protect you at home, but while you are at school you won't have anything to worry about." "My office door will always be open for you, if you feel like you are about to get into trouble or feeling overwhelmed about anything, just come in here and sit down." I still don't know how Mr. Toomer found out what happened between my family and I. Before I left out of his office, he reassured me that he meant what he said. I took full advantage of his invitation especially if I was in a class being taught by a male teacher. There were days when he would come back from lunch or monitoring the halls and I would be sitting in his office just as he instructed me to do if I had any issues. Sometimes I was written up and sent out of the class other times I would just walk out of class because he had given me the excuse to do so, so I used it.

Being a freshman in high school became an even more difficult transition adding sexual abuse, feelings of loneliness and confusion to the already heavy burdens that teenage girls carry. I had friends, but I always felt like an outcast. Most of my friends lived in two-parent homes, dressed well and their academic accomplishments in middle school qualified them for AAP classes. I lived with my grandmother, rotated the same outfits, barely escaped 8th grade without being *cut into a human steak* (her words, not mine) and took classes that offered the basic curriculum. My greatest accomplishment in ninth grade was learning how to swoop my hair enough to make a decent ponytail and cover the bald spots that I'd become ashamed of and teased about since my mother pulled my hair out with braids, beads and everything in between.

I began harboring a lot of hate, resentment and anger in my heart for a lot of people, mainly my parents. During that period of my life, my self-esteem was at an all-time low, I felt disgusted every time I looked in the mirror. I was never pleased with the reflection that looked back at me. I'd learned to mask the pain and keep a smile on my face. I could've been best described as dead but walking. Simply put, I was just going through the motions. I would go to school and sit in class, refusing to put forth any effort to complete my assignments or pass tests. If I had somewhere to run and hide there is a good chance, I would have become a statistic by dropping out of school in the 9th grade. I wasn't a dummy but making dumb decisions and being a failure is what made my teachers notice me. I spent most of my days in ISS (In School Suspension) for disrespecting teachers and administrators. Little did I know that my freshman year was setting the tone for the years to come even beyond graduation.

I received failing grades in just about every subject except for Health and Biology. Around the 4th nine weeks I would start working and doing just enough to get a "C" in my classes. I foolishly believed that if I worked hard at the end of the year, it would over power what I hadn't done in the 1st, 2nd, or 3rd nine weeks. I received my final report card for the 9th grade; I earned myself a 65/F in English and an identical 65/F in Algebra. I failed the 9th grade. The end result proved that you will never receive what you do not work for. I didn't tell anyone that I failed the 9th grade, no one was checking for my report card and I didn't volunteer to show it. There's this saying that my grandmother used to say, "Ask me no question, I'll tell you no lie." Thank goodness no one asked if I passed because I would have told a lie. No one was going to use the fact that I'd failed the 9th grade to try and keep me away from Dwayne that summer and I didn't tell my friends because I didn't want to wind up in the vicious cycle of peer judgment.

Summer 1999 came and summer 1999 went. My friends were all geared up for their sophomore year after a few weeks out of school. I however was still traveling in a maze with no compass, no gps, and no one to say go right or left. Even though I knew I was headed back to the 9th grade. I started the year off with more momentum and with all intention to do the *right thing*. I was going to all of my classes, not receiving as many written referrals and completing assignments. After a while doing the right thing, felt so wrong. By then I had a reputation with the administrative staff and my teachers. I was determined to uphold that reputation as a lost child. It wouldn't be long before I slipped into my old behavior patterns of not caring about the outcome of my actions. I came up with a goal I thought to be obtainable. I wanted to be popular if nothing else.

My looks weren't going to do it, my academics surely weren't the way to reach my goal, and I couldn't be further from athletic. I wasn't on the band, although I did audition to be a flag girl, but it didn't end so well when I hit the captain with the flag pole because I didn't like her attitude. I implemented my plan by disrupting class every chance I got. My classmates knew exactly who I was once I started getting thrown out of class every other day while they laughed at my ignorance. Earning the name, "Ghetto Eb," from the varsity cheerleaders was proof that my plan to be popular was working. I liked all attention, even the negative attention. My mission was accomplished. Everyone knew me except for me. I was a stranger in my own life.

ജ‍ഇ

Everyone knew me except for me. I was a stranger in my own life.

The end of the year was approaching a lot faster than I could keep up with. My grades on average weren't as bad as the previous year. I was passing in more than two subjects. I made some progress in Math ending the year with an 80/C. My English grade hadn't budged from a 65/F. I manage to fail the 9th grade for a second time. When I failed the second time I had to tell someone because I needed to be rescued. I needed someone to pay for summer school classes. I needed to take one English course and one Math course to catch back up with my class. Of course my grandmother made a way just as she always had. She agreed to pay for me to take one of the courses in summer school because she couldn't pay for both. My guidance counselor Ms. Johnson created a plan that allowed me to take one of the subjects in summer school while having to double up on the other subject the following school year. I chose to take math in summer school, because I hate solving equations, especially when letters are added into the formula. There was no way I was taking two math courses in the same school year.

Since passing math in summer school, I was offered a bit of a second chance. Well, a third chance for anyone that may be keeping count. I was promoted to the 10th grade and was an official member of the Class of 2003. I was no longer taking classes with the class I entered high school with. However, I still spent time with my friends during lunch and after school. We even started a group, naming ourselves the SBC (Sassy but Classy) Girls also known as the 722 Girls. The numbers and letters corresponded on the dial pad of the telephone. I don't know for sure whose idea it was initially, but knowing those girls, my vote would be that D'Jaris was the mastermind. She has always been a creative and a really good friend. The type of friend where there was never a dull moment around and one that would let me borrow her shoes occasionally so that I could be half as fashionable as she was. We stayed by each other's side making good and bad decisions together, and holding tight to each other's secrets, until I fell victim to the sweet talk of "Yellow Boy" the nickname of Keenan High School's quarterback.

If I regret anything from high school, it would be the altercation in the hallway that ended our rock solid friendship, but the desire to be validated by a 16 year-old boy and using "Yellow Boy" to help me get over Dwayne meant more to me than having a friend did at that time. I was grateful that the other 722 girls didn't choose sides. Although I distanced myself away from the group once they were starting to partake in activities that upperclassmen were privileged to do. I was no longer on their level. Yet that was still my little secret. I started befriending some of the girls from my *new* class, in particular a girl name Monisha that lived in the same neighborhood as me.

I spent the next year and a half playing catch up. I was running out of time to actually graduate with my class. Ms. Johnson mapped out a plan that was going to require all of, a plan so genius that when I picked up my high school transcript, there was no indication of me ever being in the 11th grade. I had to buckle down. My class may not have noticed that they left me behind as long as we were still in school, but I'm pretty sure that they wouldn't have missed my name not being announced at graduation. I was not going to carry that embarrassment, but I still wasn't all in. My education just wasn't a priority and I had a hard time forcing it. I still spent majority of my days in Mr. Toomer's office or still showing up to the school on days I was suspended and catching the bus to Heyward Career Center with my cousin Johnny.

There were a few more caring adults at Columbia High around

the time I really needed to start focusing on graduation. One went by the name of Ms. Gaines. She was my math teacher. She took a liking to me as she guided me through my last two math classes. I remember three things about Ms. Gaines; she had a very unique spelling to her first name, which in its most common spelling is "Natasha". She was always smiling and welcomed me with opened arms whenever I interrupted her lunch breaks when I needed to vent. She also helped me to believe in myself. The other caring adult was Ms. Breland who was hired to teach English. Ms. Breland had a reputation for being a really strict teacher, but she made me want to actually learn in her class and was the most influential teacher I had at Columbia High. I remember her literally compiling information for my final senior research project for me. All I had to do was wear my black business casual attire and present it in front of a panel of individuals that had already counted me out. Mr. Toomer and Ms. Johnson now had help in getting me to my graduation on time.

I earned passing grades in both English and Math, but there were a few more *boxes* that needed to be checked off the list in order for me to become eligible for graduation. I had one more opportunity to take the South Carolina Exit Exam and I needed a passing grade in a foreign language. I tried French my second 9th grade year and lasted about a month before I threw a book at a student that ended up hitting the sweet elderly French teacher, Madame Hall. She told Mr. Toomer I was no longer allowed in her classroom. Third time was a charm for me with the exit exam. I walked in the room to give it one last shot. I was instructed to sit in the desk beside the guy that was on the radar to be recognized as the valedictorian for the class of 2003. "Hook line and sinker", I thought to myself as I knew we were about to pass that exit exam with flying colors. I'm pretty sure it appeared to be a miracle to anyone that compared my scores from that test to the scores of the two exit exams I'd failed prior. It was indeed an act of God. There was one more obstacle to cross, when Ms. Johnson did a final check on my grades, I was failing Spanish. I could not *walk* without a foreign language. Our principal went to the Spanish teacher personally one Friday afternoon and said to her, "You have to pass Ebony, she has to go."

When we returned to school on Monday, Ms. Johnson called me into her office and asked if I ordered a cap and gown because graduation was in a few weeks. We both cried. Thankfully, I had ordered a cap and gown just in case. Looking at it hanging behind my room door everyday was my first experience with the Law of Attraction as I imagined myself wearing it at graduation. Ms. Johnson was the epitome of the difference just one caring adult can make in a child's life. (She single handedly influenced my concern for teenagers of today) Kenya Johnson, grabbed a misguided teenager, committed to loving me and fulfilled her promise to get me to my high school graduation. The day arrived that I would receive my high school diploma, as we marched in; I begin to sing to myself the lyrics of Mary Mary's song "Can't Give Up Now." That song became my life's anthem when I started listening to it every day of my 12th grade year.

When my name was called, I walked across the stage shaking the hands of the administrative staff (who were equally as surprised as I was), as the coliseum was filled with cheers and people yelling my name. As I walked back into the green room Ms. Johnson and Ms. Gaines was standing by the door waiting to hug and congratulate me. I was reaching to grab my high school diploma from Ms. Johnson when she said, "Girl, this is my diploma." I smiled and told her she can have it; just let me see my name on it. It was the most beautiful sight I'd ever seen,

ॐ

Ms. Johnson was the epitome of the difference just one caring adult can make in a child's life.

"The State Board of Education on the recommendation of state officials and the administrators and faculty of Columbia High School awards this diploma to Ebony Katrell English given on the 23rd day of May **2002**!" That was my last time seeing Ms. Johnson and Ms. Gaines, but I knew their purpose in my life had been fulfilled, although we never discussed what I was supposed to do once I left the coliseum after graduation.

6

LOVE AT FIRST SIP

Ebony K. English

As high school came to an end, I was so focused on catching up with my class that post-graduation plans were never a thought. I wasn't one of those students privy to the conversations about college. No one spoke to me about what was next. In their defense my 1.959 G.P.A and 115 of 140 class ranking hadn't really earned me a seat at the table to have those conversations. I did just enough to accomplish the only real goal I had which was graduating from high school on time. I sat around the house hopeless, with no dreams, goals or job while waiting on my friend Monisha (Mel) to graduate the next year.

I was hoping she would have some plans on what we were going to do next. Shortly after her graduation she came to my house one day in July of 2003 really excited that she was accepted into Benedict College. Totally oblivious to the process of going to college, I said to her "Girl I'm going to Benedict too." I'd forgotten that me and four of my cousins received trespassing warnings from Benedict's campus police the year prior for fighting. I was guilty by association, I'm a lover not a fighter. I'd also forgotten that I didn't have the minimum 2.0 G.P.A. No college was going to accept me. Mel encouraged me to apply although I also missed the application deadline too. I filled out an application, turned it in to the admissions office along with my high school transcript and prayed that my 1.959 G.P.A was enough to make me a *Tiger*. A week after submitting my application, I received a letter from the best HBCU (Historically Black College and Universities) in all the land that read; "Congratulations you have been accepted into Benedict College." To my surprise barely meeting the prerequisites didn't matter to the "higher learning institution of second chances." I was officially a college student. A college student with no plan, but nonetheless a college student.

The only real idea I had of college was what was portrayed on *A Different World* and *The Cosby Show*, but I would learn more as I embarked on my own personal journey. Less than a month later, I was moving in on campus. Although I am from Columbia, the same city that the college is located in, it made sense for me to live on campus because I did not have transportation to and from class. Besides, if it was an opportunity for me to get out of the apartment with my mother, I was on the first thing smoking out of there. I took all my B2K posters off of my wall at my mom's house, packed up everything that I could and transported my stuff to the campus.

As we pulled up to the dorm I noticed there were cars full of people dropping off girls from everywhere, different walks of life, and experiences all hoping to make something of themselves at a historically black college. I could barely focus on the business at hand because the football players were out in droves assisting with move-ins. The dorm director Ms. Mills greeted all of us at the front door. She wasn't just a dorm director; she was the mother away from home for every one of us that would be living in the dorm under her supervision. She did not take her job or responsibility lightly, it was obvious that she was not there to play games with us.

Once I completed all of the official move-in documents, Ms. Mills issued me my room assignment and key. Room 604 in Mather Hall is where I would begin my college lodging. She explained all the rules of the dorm, but the two that she emphasized the most were: Visitation from the opposite sex was prohibited as well as entering the dorm after the 12:00 am curfew. My mother laughed as she said, "You haven't had a curfew all of your life, you come to college and now you're being told what time to come in." I could see the humor in that, but it went in one ear and out of the other. Rules rarely applied to me unless I created them myself. We took the elevator up to the 6th floor and found room 604. My new roommate was already in there with her sister and mother getting her things arranged to her liking.

"Hey, what's your name?"

"Tionna"

"Oh ok, where are you from?"

"Augusta, Georgia"

"I'm Ebony, I am from here. Good ole' Columbia."

That may have been the only time that either of us called the other one by our first names. That was my first ever roommate, and that's how we referred to one another. Roommate! When our parents left, we used that time to get to know each other better, we were now sharing the same space for at least the next nine months. I asked her did she like B2K because I had tons of posters that I wanted to use to decorate our walls. She wasn't as big of a fan as I was, but she was ok with me putting a few of the posters up. I started to decorate my side of the room by spelling my name on the wall with some pictures of myself and the family and friends that I love most, and taping some posters of Omarion, (he was my favorite), right over my bed. We spent the next few days getting to know each other. She shared her goals, and I made up something for conversational purposes. I still had no idea what I was doing on a college campus.

We were all settled in, but there were still a few things that we had to do to make everything official, explore campus, complete the dreadful financial aid process and declare our majors. That Monday we spent hours in the Benjamin E. Mays Human Resource Center (the gym) to receive clearance for financial aid. When it was finally my turn to speak with a financial aid advisor, I was immediately informed of the news that if I was going to attend college I would be going strictly off of federal student loans and a GAP loan that Benedict offered, in which the fine print read your first born child and your right arm would be the form of re-payment upon completion of your college courses. In the gym that day is where I felt the mistakes of not taking my government funded education seriously. I was given the choice to apply for the loans or pack up my stuff and leave with the possibility of trying again the following semester.

I didn't know what would possibly change in my financial status from August to January, so I applied for the loans. I wanted so desperately to believe in myself and take full advantage of the opportunity to do some things differently. I decided to give myself a chance. After seemingly signing my life away for a college education, meeting my first college friends that day eased some of the anxiety I was experiencing.

All of my new friends were natives of South Carolina. Brandy from Rock Hill, her roommate Andrea from Summerville and Tiffany who always made sure that we knew she wasn't from Sumter, but Mayesville, down there by Sumter. I was introduced to them by Tiffany's roommate Santana. She and I attended middle and high school together, so I knew her very well. I introduced them to my new roommate and eventually introduced them to Mel too. There was a silent pact that we would endure our freshman year of college together.

It would be a fun filled week before the upperclassmen returned. We had parties and other events that allowed us to become more acclimated with our new environment. Benedict was a melting pot of African-Americans from all different cultures. Being from Columbia, I always heard very negative commentary about Benedict, so to meet people from all fifty states, as well as other countries caught me by surprise. Why would anyone move from California or Trinidad to attend Benedict? Up until that point everyone I'd attended school with I'd known for years. I was in a different space, with a clean slate. College was the perfect opportunity to reinvent myself. No one at Benedict knew my journey of where I came from; all they knew was what I would eventually choose to show them. They didn't have anything to make any immediate judgements by.

The first week of partying blurred my objective of even being in college in the first place. Academic achievement was put on the back burner. I struggled to find a balance between having a social life and being responsible for my academic success. I would attend classes, but failing to plan proved that I planned to fail. That time around failing would cost me thousands of dollars. There were several days that I was grateful that the college implemented the S.E.E (Success Equals Effort) policy, which a large percentage of student's grades was calculated off of attendance and an ounce of effort. It was unfair for those that actually attended class and did the work, but it worked in the favor of those students like me. I did well academically in classes that I enjoyed learning in. Others, I did the minimum of being present to be awarded a grade of C.

My freshman year of college is when I actually realized how broken I was, I was never affirmed by either of my parents. My mother never told me I wasn't good enough, but she had never told me that I was good enough either. Having no one to believe in me stripped me of believing in myself. I found it difficult to achieve because I knew that no one would be there to say, "I am proud of you." I was starving for a *pat on the back*. It never occurred to me to prove anyone wrong. I'd always accepted everything as it came. I lived a very nonchalant and careless life. If I failed, it was ok. If I lucked up and succeeded that was ok too, it didn't make a difference to me what the outcome of my decisions were.

I started carrying hundreds of dollars' worth of text books in one hand and years' worth of insecurities in the other hand everywhere I went around campus; it was only a matter of time before my lack of self-worth was sniffed out by males. Our very first college homecoming as students, Brandy met the man that would become her husband, a sigma man named Tim. Their connection was the beginning of us hanging out with the Sigmas. Ms. Mills expressed her concerns about us spending time with the Sigmas but we ignored them all. We were young adults fully capable of making our own decisions even if we would come to regret some of them in the future.

I was introduced to one of Tim's line brothers, who they called T -Mac. I called him by the name his mother gave him, Terrence. Terrence was an upperclassman from Orangeburg, SC. He and I had an instant attraction to each other. He was very funny and the life of the party. The more time we spent together, the more I wanted to be with him. Our relationship became very toxic, quickly. But, I was willing to accept a toxic relationship over no relationship at all. He would come pick me up from the dorm to spend time with him in the apartment he was living in off campus. I spent my nights engaging in sexual intercourse with him and my days thinking about when we would be together again.

ഇന്ദ്ര

Intoxication became my preferred state of being. My desire to drink increased the more I consumed it.

It was with Terrence and his frat brothers that I had my initial experience with alcohol consumption at a Sigma house party. I had a taste of "blue juice" (the fraternities' signature punch) and some other alcoholic beverages. I felt safe drinking with them. The Sigmas became like brothers to me and Brandy was always there with me; the same girl that gave me her Nautica coat when I didn't have a jacket to keep me warm in the winter months and shared her groceries with me when I didn't have anything to eat once the café closed would never allow anything to happen to me.

Intoxication became my preferred state of being. I wasn't in love with the taste of alcohol; I was in love with the feeling or the lack of feeling that it offered. My desire to drink increased the more I consumed it. I wasn't old enough to purchase alcohol at the time, but when a person is chasing a high, they will find a way to get it. I would intentionally force my way into environments where I knew alcohol would be present. Alcohol gave me the courage to say and do things that I would not be bold enough to do otherwise. It numbed all of the feelings of resentment, anger, and rejection that I was harboring in my heart. I became the life of any party I attended. My insecurities were so loud that if confidence wanted to show up, it wouldn't stand a chance. Alcohol gave me the false impression that I was finally good at something. I took pride in drinking people under the table and being *admired* for being able to hold my liquor.

ജ൙

My insecurities were so loud that if confidence wanted to show up, it wouldn't stand a chance.

The only nights I would go to the local club is when they would host their famous, "Drink or Drown" parties. I would drink until the self-defeating thoughts drowned. My preference was anything except brown liquor. As much I loved alcohol, brown liquor triggered the memory that E & J Brandy was a staple in our home, even when my mother told me she didn't have money to purchase necessities. She always could afford E & J. I felt that brown liquor was one of the reasons my needs were neglected.

Along with alcohol becoming my vice, my lack of self-respect became noticeable. My sophomore year of college, I started being very promiscuous. Terrence was still my boyfriend, but he lacked respect for me and our relationship. He would allow other girls to kiss him in front of me and then would try to make me feel delusional by telling me I didn't really see it. All of that was starting to work against him when I started getting the attention of more guys around campus and was introduced to a guy that was a student at Clemson University. I was able to juggle him and Terrence for a while because I only saw him when he came home on the weekends.

He and I lasted a few months before his sister convinced him that I wasn't worth his time. Apparently me being a Benedict College Tiger and him being a Clemson University Tiger meant that I was beneath him and didn't meet his family's standards. I'd moved to the co-ed dorms with Mel by the time I started juggling relationships. She was able to get us a room on the first floor which meant easy access through the side window. Whenever Terrence and I would have our arguments, my on-campus boyfriend would sneak in at night to fulfill my sexual desires. He and Terrence were totally unaware of the other one's existence. I only cared about one person's feelings, mine. I had a very entitled mindset and decided that somebody had to pay for the heartache and pain that my previous boyfriends inflicted upon me. I was at the point of using what I had to get what I wanted. Sharing my body was enough for me to have their undivided attention if only for thirty minutes or less.

Before I went to bed after my late night sexual encounters I would take a few shots of vodka and deal with my real feelings of unworthiness when I awoke the next morning. The built up feelings of rejection bred my obsession to be validated by men. I wanted to be chosen. I wanted for once to be good enough for someone; anyone. I wasn't picky. My promiscuous ways were less about the actual sex act and more about filling an empty void. I equated a guy's willingness to have sex with me as him wanting to love me. Those twisted thoughts created a lot of self-inflicted wounds. With every sexual encounter there was a transfer of spirits. Even when they were long gone from my bed, a piece of them stayed with me, and a piece of me went away with them. The faces changed, but the results were always the same. I was only good enough for sex. I wasn't worth keeping.

ଽଠଊ

The faces changed, but the results were always the same. I was only good enough for sex. I wasn't worth keeping.

Terrence remained my kryptonite. We were dangerously in love, no matter how much we would physically fight or betray each other with other people, we always found our way back to one another. He and his line brother "Duck" had the brilliant idea that I should pledge Zeta Phi Beta Sorority, so that we would be *bonded* for life. Even if our relationship failed we would always be "blue and white" family. I didn't have any real knowledge of any of the sororities, so their influence weighed heavily in my decision to become a member of Z Phi B. The first year I applied, I was denied because my GPA was too low. Once again finding myself working towards an isolated goal I was accepted the second time I applied along with thirteen other ladies that would become my line sisters. Zeta opened the door to new friendships, and a legitimate reason to party with the Sigmas without looking like a *groupie*.

Zeta offered me a feeling of belonging and sisterly love. Ironically, I became closest to my line sister Sheena although I used to scowl at her when I would see her around campus. Sheena became one of my best friends through Zeta even though she along with my other line sisters had their fair share of frustrations with me while we were pledging. I was very defiant. I always did things my way. Being a pledgee didn't change that. I hadn't quite grasped the understanding that we were "one line, one mind." We were all held accountable for my actions. Once our initiation process was over they all loved and seemed to forgive me for the drama I caused our entire line and together we were the 14 DOVES of Royal Blue Distinction.

A few months later after we crossed, we were attending a bonfire and bonding with newly initiated Greeks from other organizations when I looked across the yard to see a young man wearing a lavender shirt looking in my direction. I'd never seen him around campus before and was a little curious about who he was. I soon found out that he was one of the newest Kappa Alpha Psi initiates that semester. His fraternity brother by the name of Denahzio (who affectionately called me cuzzo) must have witnessed us looking at each other and took it upon himself to introduce us.

"Come here cuzzo, I want you to meet somebody."

"Ok, who is this?"

"This my frat brother, Fray."

Me: "Hey Fray."

Him: "My name is DeVonn."

Him: "I heard you just crossed Zeta."

 Me: "Yeah, how do you know?"

Him: "He just told me when I asked him who you were."

Me: "Oh, Ok and I see you're a pretty boy."

Him: "What dorm do you live in?"

Me: "I'm in Haskell, how about you?"

Him: "I live in Oak Street,"

Him: "Can I call you?"

Me: "You can."

We exchanged numbers and parted ways. DeVonn was my type; brown skin, hazel eyes, clean cut and very good looking. He was intelligent too. I later learned that he was serving as our Student Government Association's Corresponding Secretary. After three years, me and Terrence's relationship was fizzling out even though we were still trying to force it. I thought DeVonn could assist with me finally calling it quits between Terrence and I, until one of my friends dropped the bomb that he was in a relationship too. We still would spend time together riding around in his white Cadillac; the one that only allowed passengers to enter through the back seat. Everything escalated so fast between DeVonn and I that we hardly had time to get to know each other. We enjoyed a few nights of drinking and conversing before life as we knew it would become a thing of the past.

Ebony K. English

7

A NEW LIFE

Ebony K. English

I was in the fourth grade when I experienced my first menstrual cycle. Clueless as to what was happening with my body and petrified when I saw the mess in my panties and tried to sneak them in the dirty clothes basket. My mother said to me, "Let me see your panties." I screamed, "I didn't do anything wrong. I don't know what happened!" She said, "Girl, your period is on." "What is a period?" "It's something that all girls go through every month; I'm going to show you how to put on a pad when you get out of the shower." Every twenty-eight days from that day, my cycle came on like clockwork, never missing a beat until October 14th, 2006.

I was awakened that morning by every sign of my cycle, but no actual flow. I didn't worry immediately, as it felt like normal. But when I checked, I only had two pink spots. I waited for a few hours before I told Sheena, my new roommate once we moved to the off campus apartments.

"Sheena, something is definitely wrong. I've been having my cycle forever, and I've never had a problem with it being off schedule."

"I don't know girl. The way you and Fray be having sex, you might be pregnant."

"There is no way I am pregnant by him. Do you know how long me and Terrence been having sex and this never happened?"

"Those are two different people. There's only one way to find out. I will get a test for you in the morning."

I didn't sleep at all that night as should've, could've, and what ifs clouded my mind. The next day Sheena kept her word. She returned from her 8am class with a First Response pregnancy test. I asked her to sit it on the counter in the bathroom while I gathered my thoughts. I knew my body well and was pretty sure the test would be positive.

I took the test, sat it on the counter, and walked out of the bathroom to wait three minutes with my feet pacing and my heart racing. Three minutes is a long time to wait on news that could possibly change your life. Two pinks lines determined my future. Sheena and I sat silently in disbelief for a few minutes, until she asked, "So what are you going to do?" "I guess I better call DeVonn." He didn't answer. So I texted him and told him to call me ASAP. He called me as he was walking back to his dorm room.

Him: "Yo, what's up?"

Me: "I have some news. I don't know if it's good or bad."

Him: "I already know you're pregnant."

Me: "How did you know?"

Him: "I have been having symptoms. I think it happened that night we drank all that black gin." "What are we going to do?"

Me: "I guess we're going to be having a baby."

Him: "I am about to graduate next semester. This will change all of my plans. I can't have a baby."

Me: "Well what are you suggesting?"

Him: "Give me some time. I will call you back."

Me: "True."

I hung up the phone and told Sheena I was about to take a nap before I walked across the street to tell Terrence.

"Terrence?"

"Yes, Terrence"

"What does T-Mac, have to do with this?"

"Nothing. Just out of respect, I want him to find out from me sooner than later. Matter of fact, I am only giving DeVonn a few days to tell ole girl too. They both deserve to know from us before I start showing." When I woke up from my nap, there was a long list of people I had to tell; my grandmother and my aunts were all at the top of the list. I left it up to one of them to share the news with my mom.

Grandma: "You can't even take care of yourself! I would love to see you take care of a baby because I am not doing it." She said before hanging up the phone in my face. This was only the second time in my life my grandmother was upset with me. The first time was when I came home after my 18th birthday with what she called a "tramp stamp" tattooed on my lower back.

Aunt Mini: "So who you pregnant by? Terrence?"

"No, this boy name DeVonn."

"Oh so you just having sex all over the place now?"

"Not exactly, me and Terrence broke up a little while ago."

"Ok then, I'll talk to you later."

Aunt Faye: "Its ok niece. Everything is going to be alright."

Aunt Diane: "You haven't done anything that the rest of them haven't done." She was referring to my other cousins. I am the oldest of the eight of us born in the same year. But I was second to last to have a baby.

I also used my pregnancy as a reason to finally call my daddy using the number that my brother had given me years prior. I'd hoped that having a grandchild on the way would make him want to be a better grandfather than he was a father. My fingers trembled and my palms were really sweaty as I dialed the number. A part of me wished that no one answered the phone, but the other part of me wished that the news would spark a new beginning for my daddy and I. Thank goodness he answered the phone that day. I was not in the mood to argue with his wife.

"Hello?"

"Hey is this Thomas Prescott?"

"It is. Who is this?"

"This is Ebony, your daughter. How you doing?"

"Oh, I'm doing alright I suppose."

"That's good. I was calling because I wanted to tell you that you have another grandchild on the way."

"Oh ok." Then everything went silent

"Alrighty, that's all I wanted to say."

"Well Ebony, before you hang up, I have something to tell you."
My heart started to beat really fast, this was the moment I've been waiting for all my life. I just knew he was going to say that he wanted a relationship with me. I couldn't have been more wrong.

"Thank you for sharing your good news with me, but I've had some time to think over the years and I just don't believe that you're my daughter. See, your mother gave birth to you in March; early March. And from the last time she and I were together, you should have been born in April. I'm sorry. Hopefully you will find out who your daddy is soon."

"Thank you for sharing that with me, I am sorry to have bothered you."

The phone call surely didn't go as planned. I called with the news that I'd hoped would bring us together only to receive a bomb that would push us further apart. Sheena sat on the edge of the bed beside me as I fought back tears. I didn't have time to sulk. After all, I couldn't miss something that I never had and I needed my energy for one last order of business. I still had to tell Terrence.

It was later that evening when I finally had the courage to walk over to his room. He opened the door and greeted me like he always had.

"What's going on Piggy?"

"Can I talk to you in your room?"

"Come on."

"I started to text you, but I thought it would be better to tell you face to face. I just found out today that I am pregnant." His eyes filled with tears. I'd never seen those types of emotions from a man before. I felt so small. I may have hurt the only man that cared about me. In that moment it didn't matter how toxic our relationship was. His heart was shattered.

He said, "And I bet you pregnant by that lil pretty boy Kappa you claimed you weren't messing around with. That's supposed to be my baby."

"It is him and I am so sorry."

"Sorry won't change a thing Piggy. Good luck."

I didn't cry until I was back in my room. Terrence didn't speak to me for months, anytime we were around each other handling Zeta/Sigma business, he would look at me in disgust or not look in my direction at all. I understood his pain. I would have felt the same way had he impregnated another girl weeks after we ended our three-year relationship.

The following morning once everything settled, I stayed in bed evaluating my life. I was twenty-two years old and pregnant. That wasn't too young. But it was too young to be bringing another human into the world without a solid foundation. I was barely responsible enough to make it to my classes on time. I was the girl that didn't feel comfortable holding babies until they were old enough to hold their heads up on their own. I didn't know the first thing about being a mother. Nothing had prepared me. Not even the parenting education class I took in high school prepared me for the reality that I was a mother to be. I went to bed that evening without hearing anything from DeVonn. I figured he needed some time to digest everything. It was definitely a situation that needed to be chewed in bite size pieces. I was willing to give him his space.

Two days later, DeVonn returned to my room carrying a piece of paper in his hand. The look on his face was one of disappointment, so I asked if he was ok. He said, "I can't have a baby right now and neither can you. So I have found some organizations that will assist with an abortion."

He handed me the paper he was holding onto and left. I never looked at what was written on the paper. I folded it up and placed it in the white Bible that my sorority sisters gifted me when I crossed Zeta. Whatever was on that paper was between him and God. I knew that an abortion was not an option. I was in desperate need of support, so I sent a mass text to all of my friends and another one to my line sisters to let them know that I was pregnant. I also called my favorite cousin Sheria (who had just given birth earlier that year) to ask her if she knew of a good doctor and if she could take me to my first appointment. Without hesitation, she recommended the doctor that delivered her daughter. As we arrived to my doctor's appointment a week later, I sat nervously in the waiting room, asking Sheria every question I could think of. She said, "This appointment is easy. They will collect a few tubes of blood to confirm the pregnancy and test for any sexually transmitted diseases. They'll also do an ultrasound, and you will probably be able to hear the baby's heartbeat."

"Already?"

"Yes, already."

I was called back into a room by a medical assistant. She checked my vitals and administered the blood tests. We sat in the room for about twenty-five minutes waiting on the official results. The next person to enter the room was a black woman wearing a white lab coat with the warmest smile on her face.
"Ms. English?"

"Yes ma'am"

"I am Naomi, the nurse practitioner. How are you doing?"

"I am doing ok. How are you?"
"I'm doing pretty good. I have your test results, and it appears that you have been doing some *juking* (her word for having sex). Your pregnancy test is the only one positive. All of the STD tests are negative."

"That's a relief. I'm not trying to leave with a prescription for a STD."

"Thank God, because I am not trying to write you a prescription for a STD."

We both laughed.

"We are going to get you an ultrasound so that we can determine how far along you are and your due date. Congratulations!"

"Thanks, I guess..."
She hugged me and assured me that everything was going to work out according to God's will. She informed me that my doctor was a black man by the name of Dr. Smith, and together they would take great care of me on my journey to motherhood. Her pleasant persona earned my trust. Once the ultrasound determined that I was a little over five weeks pregnant with the due date of June 20th, 2007 she helped me sit up and handed me the sonogram photos. She explained that my appointments would be monthly, then bi-weekly, and would eventually become weekly as it got closer to my due date. The verdict was in, I was undoubtedly pregnant.

Given our new reality, the father of my unborn child and I had some decisions to make. I didn't have time after my appointment though. I had to prepare to represent as Miss Zeta Phi Beta in the Miss Benedict coronation. DeVonn was my escort and dance partner for the event. While we were dancing, I kept asking if I looked pregnant and if he thought anyone would notice. He'd let me know that it was too early for anyone to notice and reminded me that I had already told everybody. He and I finally got a chance to sit down after coronation to discuss future plans. I told him that I would never be able to forgive myself if I had an abortion. It was a long heated conversation filled with a lot of emotions. The end result was we were in our last year of college and would soon be entering into a *class* that neither of us registered for. Parenting.

Once we made that decision, he started to tell his family. I wasn't sure if he told his ex-girlfriend. So I took it upon myself to do one of the most obscene things I have ever done in my life. I compiled all of the maxi pads and tampons that I had, put them into a Dollar General bag, went to the shuttle stop, and waited until she drove into the apartment complex. When I saw her car coming around the corner, I waved her down signaling her to stop. She stopped and rolled her window down. I asked if DeVonn told her the news. Before she could answer, I interjected, "Girl, I'm pregnant." I proceeded to give her all the sanitary napkins and said, "You can have all of them. I won't need any for at least nine months." I was so disappointed in myself once it was done and I couldn't take it back. How distasteful was it for me to spew hatred into her already open wounds.

The pregnancy affected DeVonn and I differently. With him being the more ambitious of the two of us, it motivated him to work harder academically so that he could graduate and obtain a good job. I had the opposite reaction. I continued going to class until I started showing. Then I became a little self-conscious and started to spend most of my time at the apartment, locked away in our room. I managed to put myself on bed rest demanding Fruit Loops every other day. I had the cravings. He had the sickness.

Sheena and I became very frustrated with one another because every time she came to the room, I was in there. She never had a chance to be alone and at night she had to deal with me and DeVonn. Once he fully accepted that I was pregnant, he rarely stayed away from me long enough to make me feel like I was alone.

However, the reality of me not using the pregnancy as a reason to get myself together disturbed him. I wouldn't be surprised if he felt conceiving with me was the biggest mistake of his life. Aside from the normal stresses of pregnancy, I am sure having a child on the way by a girl that was only good for counting down to the days until she would be able to drink again added more disappointment.

Everyone wanted more for me than I wanted for myself. Sheena's boyfriend brought me assignments from our classes and I would just sit them on the desk to collect dust. Our housemates would always make sure I ate. Brandy assisted with getting me to my doctor's appointments and Mel made sure that I never felt like I didn't have a friend. I was so inactive that I only left the room to eat, go to the doctor, or attend Zeta meetings. I only attended meetings because I wanted to make sure that Mel was voted in and that the girl who kissed Terrence in front of me was rejected.

In February of 2007, the time finally arrived for us to find out the sex of our child. Of course DeVonn wanted a son. It didn't make a difference to me one way or the other. On the day of the ultrasound, the baby's legs were wide open and there was no doubt that we were having a baby boy. That was probably the first time I witnessed DeVonn remotely close to being excited. Once the sex was determined we were then faced with the task of naming our son. DeVonn didn't want a junior, but thought it would be cool for them to have the same middle name and last name. I fell in love with the name Dallas. I thought that it was a very unique name and went well with Jamar and Fray. DeVonn hated the name, but he let me down gently and suggested Jaden. I didn't like Jaden. He thought about it for a while and came up with the second most common name for baby boys born in 2007. Jalen. I loved the name, but I told him it had to be spelled differently than all the other variations of the name. I spelled out the letter J (Jay) and added another 'L', that way I could somehow feel like we at least had a part of the name Dallas. My explanation was quite comical to him, but by the end of the night, our son had a name, Jayllen.

With the name checked off of our list, the next important thing was the selection of Jayllen's godparents. I left the selection of godfather up to DeVonn. There was only one person *perfect* for the role of godmother, Mel. I was so excited to ask her to be the godmother to my unborn child. Aside from my blood relatives, I knew she would take amazing care of my son in my absence and guide him on the journey to accepting Jesus Christ as his Savior. When I approached her about it, she wasn't quite as ecstatic as I'd hoped she would be. It wasn't as though she wouldn't have loved to, her cancer had returned and I wasn't aware. Mel was a soul so full of life that she would never tarry in negative energy. Me on the other hand, I have never been a good person to share bad news with. I am a worry wart and tend to internalize my loved ones pain. She knew that about me which is why I probably didn't know how aggressive her cancer had gotten until the moment she suggested that we ask her older sister, Shuana, to be Jayllen's godmother. I took heed to what that must have meant, and obliged. Shuana was more than honored to take on the role as God Mommy.

Mel being committed to do all she can in spite of her illness, along with my other friends, hosted the most amazing baby shower. We were in college, but my friends did not spare any expense on gifts. I was expecting pampers and wipes. Imagine my surprise when my college mates attended the baby shower with car seats, strollers, pack & play, limited edition Dr. Seuss books and "Future Kappa" paraphernalia in addition to the bare necessities. We were so fortunate that when my family called to ask me what we needed, all I could say was "a place to live." That was more than anyone could afford, and my room and board did not cover a new born child. DeVonn was applying for jobs in Columbia, as his graduation date was drawing near.

Employment was not guaranteed and neither was housing for any of us. The closer it got to my due date, I stopped going to all of my classes. Withdrawing from them would have put me in a better position, but that wasn't the decision I made. My final grades that semester were three F's and one C. My female instructors refused to attend my pity party and accept my excuse of being pregnant and nearly dead due to my battle with depression. One of them even said to me that she didn't care about any explanation or excuse that I had because she didn't get me pregnant and I wasn't her problem. My only male instructor wanted so desperately to help me when I didn't have enough sense to help myself. But there was nothing his gift of a C could do for my G.P.A. I was officially a failure with a dependent on the way. DeVonn received his degree in May of 2007 and less than a month later; our lives would never be the same.

On June 4th, 2007 I went to what ended up being my final

doctor's appointment. Dr. Smith checked my cervix only to realize that I hadn't dilated. He scheduled me to be admitted into the hospital on Sunday June 10th so that he could induce my labor. On Sunday, DeVonn arrived to my grandmother's house wearing a shirt that said, "I am the daddy." He was prepared. Meanwhile, I was falling apart. I walked down the side walk slowly feeling like my knees were buckling with every step. I turned around to face my grandma and burst into tears, crying hysterically, "Grandma I am afraid to have a baby." "You should've thought about that before you got pregnant. The baby is in there now, he has to come out." I wasn't used to my grandmother's love being *tough*, but I knew if it was anything she could do to save me, she would have given it her all to do so. There was no turning back.

After being checked into my hospital room that evening Dr. Smith rechecked my cervix, I still hadn't dilated. He ordered the nurse to come in to administer a single dose of Pitocin to promote labor induction. I waited hours for the effects. I didn't experience anything. I told DeVonn maybe it will work if I went to sleep. About 7:50 am the next morning, I woke up and still hadn't experienced any contractions. Dr. Smith came into the room, checked my cervix and was surprised to realize that the Pitocin did not work. "Your cervix hasn't done anything" He said with a puzzled look on his face.

"What is going to happen now?" I asked.

He proceeded to check my blood pressure, looked over at the nurse and said, "Let's prep the OR."

Confused, I asked, "What's the OR?"

"It's the operating room Ms. English. You're going to have a C-section."

30 Seconds later, approximately five healthcare workers ran into the room, all of them doing something different. One was shaving, one was having me sign papers indicating all of the possible complications that could occur, one inserting a catheter while saying, "You're going to feel a little pinch but you can handle it. You're about to be a mother," and then there was the anesthesiologist. Everything was happening so fast.

Frantic, I blurted out "I can't have surgery. I have never had surgery and my grandmother is not here."

DeVonn: "It's ok Eb. I am here."

"You are not my grandmother. Pass me my phone so that I can call my grandma."

"Grandma, these people are trying to take me to have a C-section. I didn't even have time to think about it."

"What time are they doing it?"

"They are rolling me back now."

"Oh no baby, I will be there as soon as my cab gets here."

We both started to cry, but couldn't stop the procedure. Moments after being rolled into the operating room, Dr. Smith said, "Alright Ms. English, it's time. You will feel a lot of tugging and pressure. If there is any pain, please let us know."

The actual procedure took approximately thirty-five minutes. The topic of discussion around the operating table was how the Cleveland Cavaliers were about to get swept by the San Antonio Spurs in the 2007 NBA Finals. Two things happened in that operating room on Monday, June 11th 2007. I was indirectly influenced to learn more about the Phenom that we now know as LeBron James, I have been his biggest fan ever since. Most importantly I became a mother to Jayllen Jamar Fray. He entered this world at 8:38 am weighing 6lbs and 9.5oz. One look at my son and the fears of not knowing how to be a mother vanished.

8

UNEXPECTED

Ebony K. English

As much as I wanted to be happy that my healthy baby boy had finally made his arrival, I was too focused on the dilemma that we still did not have a guaranteed place to live. As my family and friends filled my room and made their visits to the nursery to welcome the newest addition to our family, my heart rested in a sunken place. I was already failing my child and he was only a couple hours old. Aunt Diane eventually stopped visitation telling my friends that I needed to rest. I did need all the rest I could get; especially while the nurses were caring for Jayllen. I rested that first evening only to awake the next morning in excruciating pain. The doctor's ordered that I walk, pass gas, and have a bowel movement before they would allow me to go home. I was able to do two of the three, afraid I would rupture my incision if I forced a bowel movement. So I never made an attempt. I wasn't in a rush to leave the hospital. I didn't have anywhere to go. The doctors grew weary of my refusal to cooperate and discharged me anyway.

By the time I was discharged from the hospital, my mother extended an offer for Jayllen, DeVonn, and I to come stay with her since all of the gifts from the baby showers were already at her house. It wasn't the most ideal place to live, but it beat not having anywhere to live at all. I respected DeVonn for staying the course with us. He'd already accomplished what he came to South Carolina for. He could have easily packed up his belongings and moved back home to Marietta, GA but he didn't. He embraced his fatherly responsibility and pressed forward. I wish that my motherly instincts were activated immediately, but they weren't. I spent the first month in the house battling postpartum depression and wishing I had a *Parenting for Dummies* book. I didn't know how to care for a newborn baby and lacked enthusiasm for learning how to. There was one time two of my aunts popped up at the house in the same manner that a social worker and a case manager would. They kept knocking while I looked through the blinds refusing to allow them in to see how badly I was failing at motherhood. I finally let them in because they seemed to have more time to knock than I had patience to ignore them. As soon as I let them in, Aunt Mini reached for Jayllen and sniffed his neck only to say

"Why doesn't he smell like a baby?"

"Probably because I don't know what a baby is supposed to smell like."

"Baby powder, baby lotion, *baby* anything."

I took note of that lesson. Jayllen was never caught *not* smelling like a baby ever again, especially not around Aunt Mini.

Spending that first month in the house alone gave me ample opportunity to figure out what was next for my son and I. DeVonn was only in Columbia with us for a few weeks before being hired by a company that moved him to North Charleston, South Carolina. I decided that I was going to re-enroll back in college two months after Jayllen was born. There were a few obstacles I had to cross before I could commit to being a full time student and a full time mother. I was not a licensed driver. Nor did I have anyone that could be permanent transportation for me to campus and for Jayllen to my grandmother's house, since she agreed to babysit him during the day as long I was doing something productive. Brandy, being the great friend that she is, proposed that if I could pass the driver's test, she would assist with transportation by lending me her car between classes or on days when she didn't have class.

She arranged for Mel to use her car to take me to test for my driver's license for a 3rd time. Mel must have been my good luck charm. I finally passed the test. I was 23 years old with a baby before earning a driver's license. Since I passed the driver's test, I went to enroll back in school the same day. I completed the necessary documents and received my "admit to class" stamp. I was starting to feel responsible again until I shared the news with my mother. In which, she shattered all the hope I had to continue my college education. "I don't know why you did that. Y'all have to leave."

I didn't believe that putting Jayllen and I out was a decision she made. I knew her boyfriend was the mastermind. She was just the messenger. An argument ensued between the two of us as I gathered all of our clothes and placed them into plastic grocery bags. I used that opportunity to voice my frustrations about how she had always chosen a man over me and that she didn't ever have to worry about seeing me or her grandson again. "I have a responsibility to protect my child from any hurt harm or danger. That's something you wouldn't know anything about doing. You will not inflict the same pain on him as you have on me." Were my final words before leaving her house. Some may say that my motherly instincts were finally kicking in, but my intentions were to hurt her just as she hurt me.

I caught a ride to my grandmother's house to pick Jayllen up. When she saw me walking up the sidewalk she questioned why I had so many bags with me, and I told her, because my mom put me and my baby out of her house.

"Eb, I don't have anywhere to put all of this stuff"

"I just need somewhere to put my things temporarily. I have already called DeVonn to come pick us up. We are moving to Charleston with him."

"How are you going to go to school from Charleston, Ebony?"

"I'm not going back to school. Having a roof over our heads is more important right now."

"I'm so sorry baby."

"It's all good grandma. I know if there was anything you could do, you would." Tears streamed down both of our faces.

It would be a few hours before DeVonn was able to come pick us up. By 10pm, we were residents of North Charleston, living in an Intown Suites on Rivers Avenue. Living in an extended stay hotel was a humbling experience. We had great intentions to operate as a unit. However, living in those close quarters quickly made us realize that there were consequences to having children with people you barely know. DeVonn and I didn't have anything in common. He was ambitious. I was lazy and dreamless. He was business minded. I had an impoverished mindset. Our differences drew a wedge between us. He had a controlling spirit. I was uncontrollable. One day during one of our heated arguments he told me that "no one will ever want to be with me because I always had an opinion." It became very clear that we were two totally different individuals that just happened to procreate together.

Our opposite personalities failed to attract. We would spend our days parenting in shifts. He worked his corporate job during regular business hours and I worked from 6pm to close at a nearby Taco Bell. In the rare times that we were off at the same time, I would spend the day wishing that one of us had to work. Our dislike for each other was very evident and hate was on the horizon towards him. I fell into the abyss of self-sabotaging behaviors because I simply no longer wanted to be attractive to him. On nights when I drove to work, I would stop by the store to purchase a beer, a Four Loko, or anything I could guzzle really fast before I got back to the extended stay, just in case we happened to have sex. With a little help, I could pretend to enjoy it. That was only a temporary fix. I needed to come up with a permanent solution. Remembering one of our earlier conversations, I was reminded that he has never been nor would he ever be attracted to "fat" girls. I took that information and ate my way to unattractiveness forcing nearly 270 pounds on my 5'4" frame with all intention to become someone that he wouldn't have any urge to touch. The more the numbers on the scale went up, the more my self-esteem went down. I would look in mirrors only to realize I barely recognized my own face. I simply did not love myself enough to know that harming me proved what he already thought about me; I was weak minded.

While I was in Charleston fighting my own demons, life as usual was going on in Columbia for my family and friends. I rarely called home because I hadn't quite mastered "sounding happy" and I didn't want to be forced to lie when asked how I was doing. I communicated with my friends via text message. That way my tone and emotions were hard to detect. We lived in North Charleston for six months. Between visiting Mel and holidays I may have visited home four times. Visiting Mel in the hospital in October of 2007 was the first time I'd seen her since July of that year, and I had no idea that her health was declining. Her spirit was always high and she sounded great on the phone. Seeing her that day put everything into perspective for me. When we walked in the room, she was sitting up. She drifted in and out of sleep, but was still very much aware of what was happening around her. The weight and motion of me placing Jayllen in her arms caused her to open her eyes just enough to see what was going on as she said, "Hey My Jayllen Hey." She used all the strength she had to speak those four words. I still sometimes reference him with, "My Jayllen." It's not to claim ownership because everybody obviously knows he is mine. "Hey My Jayllen Hey," were the last words that I heard my best friend say.

When we returned to Columbia the following month on Thanksgiving Day, we went to visit Mel again. That time she was sedated and surrounded by family. They had all gathered to have Thanksgiving dinner at the hospital, which caused me to worry. Prior to arriving at the hospital DeVonn told me that we couldn't stay long because we had to get back to Charleston before it got too late. I wanted to be considerate of his plans to get us back *home*, so I kept my visit with Mel short and sweet. I just held her hands for a few minutes, kissed her forehead and told her that I loved her. I hugged Shuana and told her I was going to try to come back to see Mel as soon as possible. I left the hospital and rode back to Charleston in silence and feeling uneasy. We were about 45 minutes away from the Intown Suites when my phone vibrated. I look down to see that it was Shuana calling me. I sent the call to voicemail and turned my phone off. I was prolonging hearing the reality of what I already knew was coming. As I was preparing myself to call Shuana back, DeVonn's phone started to ring. It was Brandy. All I heard him say was, "Dang, I will tell her." He hung up the phone grabbed my hand, "Brandy just said that..." I interrupted him, begging him to not finish his statement. "I already know Mel died." I said through the lump in my throat. The only decent response he could come up with was "Alright. I know that was your best friend, but don't use that as an excuse to keep eating the way you have been." His insensitivity left me speechless for the remainder of the drive.

Once we arrived back to the extended stay hotel, he carried Jayllen in while I stayed outside to catch some fresh air and take a few deep breaths before calling Shuana back. As soon as she answered, we both just started to cry. I wanted so desperately for her to tell me a different story. Her inability to say anything other than, "You were the hardest person for me to call," revealed the unimaginable. My favorite girl in the world passed away on Thanksgiving Day 2007 at the age of 22. I'd lost the only person I could have a conversation with using only my eyes; my partner in lip reading and laughing out loud when everyone else around us remained confused; my pillar of strength; my sane voice. The only person I knew whose friends fought for her friendship, because she had a way of making everybody feel special. The days that followed were a blur. The one memorial service that I can clearly recollect was hosted by Zeta Phi Beta Sorority, Incorporated.

On the evening of Mel's memorial service, Grad chapter members barricaded the doors blocking access to the memorial service from all members whose membership dues were past due. I was one of the members that was asked to exit while my best friend's casket was surrounded by our sorority sisters that couldn't tell her middle name from her first name. But because their dues were current, they were allowed to memorialize a life they didn't know. Right on the outside of the door leading to the sanctuary I decided I would no longer be an active representative of Zeta Phi Beta Sorority.

I thought I'd join a sisterhood a year prior, only to be hit with the reality I had joined another money hungry organization; at least in the Southeastern region. Deny me access from chapter meetings, conferences, or the Zeta house; not from my best friend's memorial service. That was the perfect recipe for kicking a sister when she's already down. My line sisters talked me out of renouncing all affiliation to the sorority. However, I found peace in boxing up all of my paraphernalia and giving it away. The only things I kept were my crossing gifts from Mel.

I coped well as long as I was around people. It was once I was alone with my thoughts and memories of my friend that her death seemed to start choking the life out of me. I distanced myself. The thought of losing another person paralyzed me for months and kept me from getting close to new people or closer to the friends I already had. I didn't want any other friends. I wanted Monisha Melodie Davis. She now visits me in my dreams warning me about people, places and things that she and I have never discussed in the natural. I can't lay eyes on her and neither can I touch her. But even in her death one thing still remains the same, she has my back and because of her, I believe in Angels.

9

THE SHIFT

Ebony K. English

A month after Mel passed away Jayllen and I began phasing out the Charleston era of our lives. It was time for me to move back home to Columbia to replenish the love and positive energy that I lost in Charleston. It was my Christmas present to myself that year. I hadn't been close to my family for a while. I needed them: the gatherings, the laughs, the love, and all the hugs I could get. I didn't have a clear path of getting back to where I knew I belonged, and I was once again in the predicament of needing a place to live. In the midst of planning, my friend Ebony graduated from Benedict and decided she would reside in Columbia instead of returning to her home town of Hartsville. That was the blessing I needed. Paying the cost of rent alone was impossible for me at that time. A roommate would make it obtainable. In addition to buying me a 1982 gray Chevrolet Celebrity with burgundy interior, DeVonn also offered to pay my half of the first month's rent to help me transition.

I had to find a job with a decent hourly wage pronto. I didn't have a lot of options with a high school education and fast food experience. Discouraged, I began applying for positions with staffing agencies to no avail. Just when I was starting to lose hope, God being God placed me in the path of one of my old dorm directors from Benedict who was able to pull some strings at one of the local agencies and get me a temp to perm position at Blue Cross Blue Shield. Unfortunately, I was only working the temporary assignment for a month and a half before laziness and hangovers prevented me from reporting to work. With my absences accumulating, I was fired from Blue Cross Blue Shield and blackballed from any future employment with that temp agency.

Two months into our new living situation all of us started to experience tiny bites, itching and redness all over our skin. We were unsure of where the bites could possibly be coming from, until I lifted Jayllen from his crib one morning to find two bed bugs resting under his face. Hearing complaints from our neighbors confirmed that the apartment complex was infested with bed bugs. We felt the apartment management was knowledgeable about the infestation before we signed our lease, but they argued against ever being aware of the bed bugs. Treatment after treatment failed to rectify the problem. We decided to break our lease, take all of our clothes, leave all of our furniture in the apartment and deal with the consequences (credit issues) as they arrived. Jayllen and I moved into an apartment on Old Bush River Road. DeVonn had officially moved back to Columbia and moved into the new apartment with us. We learned in Charleston that we could not live together. Nothing changed except the city and the four walls. We were disgusted with one another. He was definitely more tolerable of me than I was of him. Everything he did would drive me crazy. We barely survived another two months parenting under the same roof before he decided to sign a lease for an apartment of his own on the other side of town. Before we separated, he made sure to tell me that I will not be able to raise our son without him.

Nothing about his comments were a surprise to me because I knew his need to be in control and if I were honest, I'd relinquished control to him. My stagnation, my lack of drive and ambition even after giving birth, gave him the confidence to believe that I wouldn't amount to anything without him. He hadn't just spoken those words; he internalized them and eventually implemented a plan to see me fail by any means necessary. Just as fast as he received the key to his new apartment, I received the first of many court orders disputing the $44.37 he was paying in weekly child support. Yes I was the poster child for government assistance. I was living in an income based apartment, and a recipient of food stamps, Medicaid, a utility assistance check and daycare voucher. However, disputing $44.37 a week showed me early on how low he was willing to go. But that was only the beginning.

He would come to visit Jayllen or pick him up to take him back to his apartment or to visit his new girlfriend in Charlotte on the weekends. I suppose he wanted me to be more bothered by his new relationship than I actually was. I was more relieved than anything. But of course I still needed the *scoop* on who she was. Through a very thorough Facebook search, I learned that she was a native of Virginia with a degree from South Carolina State University, loved bowling, and she was my sorority sister. I assumed having such an ambitious woman in his life lit his fire to the point of realizing that South Carolina's job market didn't have a whole lot to offer him with his Business & Management degree.

He started to explore his options starting with what I thought was a quick getaway to Washington DC to visit his mother, only to receive a text message that stated, "Hey I made it to DC safely, this is where I will be living now." What he did with his life was none of my business, however being left alone to raise our son was all of my business. I had no idea of the possibility of him moving to DC, but that text message was loud and clear. I sat up against the wall in Indian style and screamed so loudly that it prompted Jayllen to come into my room. He climbed in my lap and looked up at me through his light brown eyes just like his daddy's. I looked back at my one and a half year old son through my tear filled eyes and said to him, "it's just me and you baby."

He hugged my neck as if he was fully aware of what was going on, right before we fell asleep on the floor in fetal positions. When I awoke the next morning, I cleaned my face of the dried up stream of tears, and put on my proverbial cape and became Superwoman. I went to apply for a job at Burger King and was interviewed and hired on the spot. I was no longer too good for fast food. However, I was very prideful as it pertained to accepting help to care for Jayllen. I've always felt that too much help is what caused my mother to stop caring for me and my greatest fear was ending up like her. If he needed something outside of what my Burger King check or his $44.37 a week covered, I would steal it. For at least the first year that DeVonn was in DC, shoplifting was a part-time income for me. I would steal baby clothes from Burlington and other retail stores only to return them to Walmart for gift cards, so that I could purchase any variation of pull-ups, t-shirts, wipes, Garanimal outfits, shoes, alcoholic beverages, and occasionally gas if the remaining balance sufficed.

We experienced our share of evenings in the dark eating ramen noodles and *gourmet* ravioli out of the can until I got paid or could borrow enough money to pay the light bill. By the grace of God, it was never more than one night at a time. Some weeks when I was low on money, I was lucky enough that we would get together to celebrate someone's birthday or a just because family gathering and I could "borrow" $20 from five different people being sure to stay clear of the ones who had already brought into my "woe is me" story. As long as I didn't have to call DeVonn to give him any indication that I needed anything extra from him, I was unashamed about begging.

After living in DC for a few months, DeVonn had the audacity to take me to court again; this time for court ordered visitation as if I moved his son away from him. He wanted visitation every other weekend. I argued in front of the court appointed counsel that traveling from DC to South Carolina every other weekend was impossible, unless he had the time and money for it, and if he did, we needed to revisit the child support case. He was awarded visitation every other week and a few weeks out of the summer until Jayllen reached school age. We were at each other's throats for two years non-stop. I was hardly the initiator, but I had no problem retaliating. It became so agitating that it was easier getting a point through to a brick wall than it was talking to him. I was a single parent and he had more time and energy than I did to plan his attacks. When Jayllen was about three years old, I was summoned to court yet again. That court order was hand delivered to my apartment after business hours and required a signature. I knew he was playing hard ball before I even opened the folder to reveal that he wanted joint custody of Jayllen. That was the big battle. He was about to get married and his household had two nice sized incomes. On paper they were more qualified than I was to provide for him. I was terrified that I was going to lose my son. He could afford to hire one of the best child and family attorneys in the city, and I had a pro bono attorney that told me I was too passionate as if my child wasn't the offer on the table.

Our attorneys went back and forth for weeks trying to get us to agree so that we could avoid going in front of a judge. Neither one of us would fold. My attorney called me into her office to tell me, "Ebony, I admire your fight, but you have to give him something. Your stubbornness could possibly cause us to lose this." I sat up in my chair folded my arms on the desk in front of me, looked her square in the eye (Olivia Pope style) and asked her how many children did she have. In which she responded, "I don't have any children Ms. English."

"Well ma'am, I am afraid you don't understand this battle. I'm not backing down. He left his son in South Carolina. I haven't moved. I don't owe him anything. He either accepts this final offer or we will see them in court. If you can't handle it, let me know now and I will go find somebody that can." She picked up the phone to call his attorney with our final agreement. "Please inform Mr. Fray that Ms. English is willing to offer him all of the holidays except Christmas, they can alternate for Thanksgiving, the whole summer after the child's birthday and the child can come this year for Mr. Fray's wedding day." Thirty minutes later his attorney called back to confirm that he agreed with the final offer, the only difference in the agreement was his wedding day. I thought to myself he didn't really want joint custody. The feud was because he thought I wouldn't allow Jayllen to visit for his wedding day.

The ink on the visitation order was barely dry before we were within the three year range of reevaluating child support. His income had increased so much that it alarmed the child support office. They contacted me to ask was I aware and would I like to revisit the case. "Yes, absolutely." That was my opportunity for revenge. We had a court date scheduled for the following month. Which gave me just enough time for me to pull a "DeVonn" on DeVonn. I intentionally quit my 11/hr. job so that my income would be automatically calculated at minimum wage. He came to court with his duck's in a row as well and health insurance for Jayllen which helped him out tremendously. The final calculations left me with my eyes widened and almost feeling bad. But then I remembered that, with the exception of his combined ten weeks of visitation, the bulk of his parenting was financial support. I avoided making eye contact with him. I knew by the sound of his deep breaths that he was furious about the increase. When the woman got up from the desk to make copies of the documents he turned to me and said, "I won't be paying that amount for long because he is going to end up with me anyway." I didn't know what to make of his statement but I took it as a threat. I asked for a police escort to my car as I left out of the courtroom obviously anxious that afternoon.

I never shared that *threat* with anyone, but I allowed it to control my life and cause me to live in fear. I wasn't willing to admit it at

I wasn't willing to admit it at the time, but he still had mind control over me.

the time, but he still had mind control over me. What did he mean by "he is going to end up with me anyway?" Was he going to kidnap him during one of his visits? Was he going to harm me so that there would be no denying him sole custody? All of a sudden, the increase in child support didn't seem worth it if it would anger him enough to contemplate harming me. I knew the hate was thick, and the respect for one another was slim, but could his statement mean what I thought it meant. I treated it has such and became very hesitant to be out once the sun set. When I knew that I would be out at night at a family function, I would pack a bag for Jayllen and I so that we could stay overnight at someone's house. My family thought it to be a noble act of responsibility because I was always too intoxicated by the end of the night. I would tell them that's why I always came with our bags packed, so I wouldn't drink and drive. The truth is, I was paranoid and felt safer in the house with other people. On days when I couldn't afford any alcohol, I would call my "drinking partner" to bring a couple bottles for us to drink. That way I would have overnight company and alcohol to silence my worries. Nights when I was home alone, I had to push one of my couches to block the door and drink a couple glasses of wine in order to cope with my anxiety.

Skeptical about what DeVonn would possibly do next. I set out on a mission to fill all the loopholes in my single parent household. I started by enrolling at Remington College as a medical assistant student. I failed at my first attempt at college, so I granted myself permission to start over. That time I had a renewed mindset. At Remington I tapped into capabilities I never knew I had. For the first time in my life, I was a model student with a positive reputation. I was recognized for my academic excellence and was often the student that the teachers boasted about in their classes. I was the student that instructors would send other students to for assistance. I showed up early and stayed late. I was selected as a student ambassador and was given a burgundy lab jacket to wear so that the whole student body knew that I was one of the elite. I was given first dibs on the externship at a plastic surgeon's office that all of the students wanted because the doctor allowed externs into the operating room to assist him. I was grateful to witness two tummy tucks, one breast implant removal, a breast reduction, and minor liposuction procedures.

Although, I was accomplishing everything that I set out to

achieve, all of the praises and attention became too much for me to bear. I knew deep down inside that the student that was receiving all the compliments and accolades is not who I truly was. I left from school one evening to purchase three bottles of Lucky Duck wine from Walmart. The most disgusting wine I had ever tasted. But it was priced at $3.97 a bottle and it got the job done. I drank all three of the bottles that evening until I was ailing. I woke up the next morning and went to my 8:00 class. My teacher acknowledged me as I walked through the door. "Good Morning Ebony. How are you?"

"I'm drunk, that's how I'm doing. This is who I am," and I sat down in my seat. She was appalled and thrown off for the entire class. She kept me after class to have a "heart to heart."

"I understand Ebony. I am still trying to rebuild my life from a crack and alcohol addiction. It's not an unusual circumstance."

That conversation with my instructor helped open my eyes to the fact that we hardly ever think of alcoholics as high functioning individuals. Our minds automatically think of the winos that we sometimes walk pass outside of convenient stores. Contrary to popular belief, alcohol deceives CEOs and business owners just as it deceives the homeless man on the corner. The instructor that I spoke with that morning was the only instructor that used to be a doctor. A life of addiction demoted her to a level of teaching at a non-profit technical college. There I was achieving more than I ever had, and all I wanted to do was reveal who alcohol told me I was. I was an overachieving "A" student by morning and an abuser of alcohol by night.

I continued on the path to finish what I started. I was expected to finish strong and didn't want to let my instructors down. I went on to finish the program with a 3.96 GPA. If there was a valedictorian selection, it would have been me. I was, however, granted the honor to speak on behalf of the class of 2010 at graduation. I didn't tell any of my friends and family that I would be speaking at graduation. I just invited them. They had to show up to get the surprise. My grandfather passed away the same week of graduation. His funeral was held on the same day as my graduation. I remember sitting at his funeral saying to myself that I have to make something of myself before I lost the last grandparent that I had, which was my maternal grandmother. I had to leave the repass early so that I could get to graduation on time. My mother gave me

$50 and told me she wasn't coming to my graduation because she doesn't drive at night. That night I realized that it is quite difficult for some people to celebrate what they didn't contribute to. It wasn't the first time she didn't show up for me and I was positive it wouldn't be the last, but I was hurt by the poor excuse as to why she couldn't come. However, I'd worked hard for that moment I wasn't going allow anything to steal my joy. I gave the first public speech of my life that evening and received a standing ovation from some of my classmates and cheers of approval from the audience. My son witnessed his mother in a cap & gown and my grandmother was proud of me. Nothing else mattered.

10

RELAPSE

"God, I won't do it myself. But if tonight is my last night and you decide not to wake me up in the morning, it is alright with me." I said to myself as I stared off into the dark of the night on October 20th, 2011. It was officially approaching a year since I graduated from Remington and I was just fired from my first medical assistant job after receiving yet another, "less than satisfactory" employee evaluation. Sexual immorality had me *drunk* in love and my soul tied to a man who probably couldn't tell anyone my last name and had only bought me one eight count chicken nugget meal from Chick-fil-A in exchange for three years' worth of drunken sex. Yet he was about to move 2,059 miles away with my heart in tow.

Life was getting heavier, and my faith muscles weren't fully developed. I felt like the walls of the apartment were closing in on me. I'd returned to the place of darkness that I put so much effort into escaping just a year prior. I would wait anxiously on something to excite me. I wasn't moved by anything. Waking up every day was a struggle, especially when worry and anxiety kept me awake at night and hangovers made lifting my head off the pillow seem impossible.

Comparison succeeded in stealing my joy as I witnessed my friends fall in love, get married, buy houses and climb the ladder of their dream careers. I wanted what they had, but I'd failed to make the decisions they made. The decisions that I did make were catching up with me as I was starting to drown in a pool of "what ifs." Life was passing me by and anytime I would reach out to be understood I was met with, "just pray about it." I was too ashamed to admit I didn't know how to pray for myself. I only knew how to pray on the account of other people and their tribulations. There was no need to worry God when I believed depression, defeat and hopelessness was my *portion* and what I deserved.

The only thing that seemed to be going well was raising Jayllen. He was getting older and parenting required more out of me. I still hadn't found a *Parenting for Dummies* book. But what I did find was two amazing examples of a mother: my Aunt Mini and Shuana. I admired the way both of them raised their children, and I always took notes. I sifted through everything I was learning from them, applied what worked for Jayllen, and threw away the rest. They were both always just a phone call away when I needed advice, but neither of them knew they were key components in me learning how to be a mother.

Refusal to fail coupled with the lessons learned from my mommy mentors made me one of the best mothers other people knew. As you all know by now, I didn't have a healthy relationship with my mother, but I used that as fuel to become the mother I wish I had. Excuse is just a word until we give it power and I wasn't going to allow anything to be used as an excuse as to why I couldn't be a nurturing mother to my son.

From the outside looking in, I've been told that I was a pro at single parenting, but I still wasn't giving myself enough credit. I had a hard time accepting the title of single mother, because DeVonn always paid child support and I didn't want to take anything from him. But yes, I was a single mother if it is defined as one who tends to the day to day needs of a child, alone. Jayllen was near school age and I was in position to give him what I thought he needed; which was access to both of his parents. I decided that I would consider moving to DC, if I could find employment, before he started school in August. He was already in DC with DeVonn for the summer, so I needed to act quickly. It was very important to me that wherever he started school, is where he would finish school. Having gone to four different elementary schools made me value stability. I wasn't going to put Jayllen through the confusion that is attached to instability.

I started applying for Medical Assistant positions in the DMV. Responses were coming in faster than I was used to. All I was receiving in South Carolina were rejection e-mails. I was able to schedule three interviews in less than a week. I shared the news with DeVonn, but I told him there was no way I could make the drive to DC alone. Without any hesitation he purchased me a ticket to ride the Mega Bus and his mother agreed that I could stay with her. Not only for the visit, but also until I got on my feet if I did make the final decision to move to DC. I didn't share my plans with any of my family, because I was still allowing other people's opinions to dictate my life. I wanted to make that decision on my own based on how the visit and interviews went.

I knew as soon as I arrived at the bus terminal at Union Station that their heavy dependence on public transportation would overwhelm me. Where I'm from, we drive everywhere we go. I wasn't so sure that I was open to keeping track of schedules and running behind trains and buses. Yet I was still open to seeing what the DMV had to offer. I was only in the city for a few days so if nothing else I wanted to enjoy myself. I hung out with DeVonn and his wife the first night, but was sure to get in early so that I could rest up for the three interviews I had the next day. His mother took me to my first interview and praying I didn't star in my own short film, "Lost in DC." I sat through a crash course on the transportation system so that I could get to my other two interviews.

ဆဩ

I didn't share my plans with any of my family, because I was still allowing other people's opinions to dictate my life.

All three of the interviews went well and I was offered one of the positions the same day. With the news that I was offered a position came discussion of living arrangements. Jayllen was going to live with DeVonn and his wife and go to school from there. I was going to live with DeVonn's mother. She had planned to buy a partition for the living room so that I would have bed space on one half and the living room on the other half. I was ready to make my decision until my last night there when I went to visit Jayllen. When I went to lay with him, I shared that I would be leaving the next morning but, the both of us might be moving to DC. He started crying, asking can he please leave with me and said that he didn't like it there.

I had a lot of time to think on the bus ride back to South Carolina. DC had more cons than pros. I would be leaving a whole apartment to live in half of someone's living room. Jayllen and I would be living separately. I couldn't lock in for six years there, and the biggest one, I would be giving DeVonn the satisfaction of being right about what he said to me, "you will never be able to take care of him without me." Was I grateful for the opportunity to live in a different city? Yes. Would I have been miserable in DC? Yes. I weighed all options and considered how Jayllen felt and respectfully declined all offers.

When I got back to South Carolina I fell into deep depression. Although DeVonn moved away, I wanted to give Jayllen what I thought he was missing. I wanted him to have regular access to both of his parents, but not at the expense of having to uproot him from the familiarity of his own home and us living in separate households. Single parenting was starting to feel like more of a choice and I knew not having someone to "tag in" would eventually zap all of my energy. It wasn't anything that a few glasses of wine or couple shots of vodka couldn't help me get through.

I started traveling down the dark alley of binges, blackouts, humiliation and extraordinary risk. When I didn't have control of things I used alcohol to trick me into believing I did. I used it to drift off to a place where I didn't have to think about life as it was. Intoxication became my favorite place, because nothing mattered there. My moderate consumption slowly crept to two or three bottles of wine a night. Someone asked me recently "is it really possible to drink three bottles of wine a night?" in which I responded "the only reason I didn't drink five is because I didn't have two more bottles in the house with me." I became the girl that bartenders wouldn't serve anymore alcohol to because my speech slurred and my eyes blurred. I would pass out in clubs, be carried out to the car and fault others when I couldn't remember if I humiliated myself. I would wake up some mornings in places that I didn't even remember being the night before. The worse was waking up at home barely recognizing the walls I dwelled in because the whole apartment was spinning around me as I laid there confused and unable to escape the daze.

The scariest and what should have been my final moment under the influence was in response to an unanswered "Happy Birthday" text I sent to a guy. I needed to know why, well the shots of vodka I took that evening needed to know why, he ignored me. I drove to his grandmother's house to find out. I ended up going in circles on

When I didn't have control of things I used alcohol to trick me into believing I did.

a dirt road in the middle of nowhere, until I ran into a stop sign, which barely stopped me from driving into someone's house. I was lost with no cell phone service. I managed to get my car to a nearby Sonic on three tires and a rim. God sent an angel to get me and my car home that night. My memory is still failing me on who the actual angel was. I woke up the next morning to go get something to eat only to realize how damaged my car was. I called my cousin Matt to tell him what happened and that I needed a new tire and rim. He called Johnny because he was closer. Johnny came and bought two tires. I asked him, "why did he buy the second tire?" he said, "just in case you want to be stupid again." He knew me well. I was scared, but only for that moment. I wasn't impacted by the incident enough to stop drinking. I begged them not to tell anyone what happened. As far as I know Matt never said anything and Johnny took it to his grave.

Ebony K. English

11

FOUND

As the clock struck midnight on my 30th birthday; I fell into the arms of my then boyfriend who was standing against the wall. I cried out that I didn't believe I would ever live to see the age of thirty. Not only was I alive, I was unknowingly about to embark on a journey to becoming well. I wanted life to be different before I turned thirty, but I failed to put any work behind my desires, although I'd come to realize that there is no substitute for 'Doing'. I started doing the work and being true to myself by breaking up with that same boyfriend one month and twenty days later on the day after his birthday. I had never broken up with anyone before so I didn't know the correct protocol. The words that flowed from my mouth surprised me, "I

ℰℬℛ

I accepted that I was only as damaged as I allowed myself to believe I was.

know we don't have a future together, I think it's just best we end things now before we ruin each other." I no longer had a need to be validated. I'd granted random men access to my heart for entirely too long. I accepted that I was only as damaged as I allowed myself to believe I was. I didn't know that ending my relationship, would free up space for God to do the seemingly impossible in my life.

There comes a time for each of us, a definitive moment when we are forced to assess where we are, and where we are going. For me it was the third consecutive weekend in July of 2014, I decided not to attend a family function. For no other reason than my Saturdays had become well spent resting my head on defeat and wallowing around in hopelessness, also known as stuck in bed, enjoying my own pity party. My failure to show up for a fish fry, prompted Aunt Diane to tally up my "no shows" and call to check up on me. Answering the phone with my best sleeping tone, did not stop her from expressing her concern.

"Hey, what's going on with you?"

"Nothing, what made you ask that?"
"You haven't been coming around lately."

In which I would respond, "I know. I've been trying to get myself together and I want to stop drinking, but I can't do that around y'all and neither can I be my true self."

"Y'all?" As her voice began to crack. "We're your family and it hurts me to hear you say that, I love you and I am worried about you. But I don't know how to help you this time. I don't want anything to happen to you Ebony. Hopefully, you will get some help," she said before we exchanged, "I Love You's" and ended the call.

I had never heard my aunt, the very person that has always been a giant in my eyes cry as much as she did that day. Maybe she does care, but that's just one person. I thought to myself. The words, "I don't know how to help you this time," played back and forth in my mind for the next few hours. Help me? What does she mean help me? There was nothing wrong with me. The truth settled and stung for weeks. The reality was she couldn't help me. No one could help me. No one was coming to rescue me. In fact, there was a part of me that didn't want to be rescued.

A couple weeks had passed when I opened an e-mail from Ebony with the words, "Free Counseling Services" in the subject line; I realized that Aunt Diane wasn't the only person that thought I could use a little help. I am usually all for free, but the counseling services part is what lead me to forward the e-mail to some friends and family members that could make better use of the services than I ever would. Again, nothing was wrong with me. My mental default was set to denial.

That's until seeking therapy for myself was broken down for me into six simple words. "Counseling is not correction, its direction." Thanks to The Brook Church App, their founding pastor, Pastor Sim was preaching me through my dysfunction before I ever contemplated stepping foot into the church that cultivated my relationship with God. With the willingness to admit that I could definitely use some direction in my life, I reluctantly responded to the e-mail that I received to schedule a consultation with a therapist. As the old saying goes, "you have to try something new to receive something new." I was trying something new.

Still not completely sold on the idea of counseling, hesitantly I called my grandmother to ask her could she babysit Jayllen while I attended sorority meetings on Tuesdays and Thursdays. She agreed and I was off to see a shrink. Moments after walking into the first session with my therapist, I sat on the couch awaiting Ashton Kutcher because surely I was being Punk'd. How was a redhead, blue eyed Caucasian male going to help me through my African-American woman, resentment, anger and daddy issues? I remained open and honest as he started to ask the questions he needed answers to in order to assist me in doing the inner work.

He introduced himself as J. Crump, a recent graduate of the University of South Carolina.

Reading my name off a piece of paper, "What brings you here Ms. English?"

"I'm hoping that you can teach me how to forgive."

"I will certainly try."

"Please. I really need help. I want to heal." I said desperately.

There wasn't any time wasted. "I have a forgiveness exercise for us to work on," he said as he pulled out a dry erase board and dry erase markers. "We are going to color code your relationships." We will use the color blue for relationships that are great, the color black for relationships that could use improvement and the color red for relationships that you would consider to be dead." I asked him if he would allow me to save us some time. I openly admitted to having four relationships in the red and every other relationship was in the blue. I didn't have any relationships that were in the middle that would have been represented by the color black. He saw the direction in which our conversation was headed and asked for me to describe my four red relationships if I felt up to it. I didn't hesitate at all.

"The first *dead* relationship is with my dad, because there is no relationship, there is a void where a father is supposed to be."

"My second *dead* relationship is with my mom. I'm her only child, but I can hardly remember being a priority to her. I am unable to fully comprehend the lack of a relationship between a mother and her daughter."

"My third *dead* relationship is with my son's father, I hate him." Looking at the discoloration on his face, I could tell that he wasn't expecting me to be so open, so quickly. He seemed to be listening intently as I continued to elaborate on the dead relationship with my son's father before he interrupted me "I apologize for cutting you off but you previously said there were four relationships in the red, do you mind telling me more about the fourth one," I dropped my head only to mumble under my breath. My relationship with myself is *dead* also, I have adopted a lot of self-destructive behaviors that I have begun to hate myself for. I need to forgive me. I also believe that I have been abusing alcohol." He documented every word I spoke as I sat on the couch feeling relieved that I was able to share aloud the discontent I had been harboring for years. He didn't get to express a lot in our first session, but he didn't allow me to leave before giving me some "homework" to do. We started with my relationship with myself. He asked me to go home sit down in front of a mirror and share with my reflection every reason that had led to self-hatred. I didn't do my homework that evening, I was afraid to be honest with myself. I hadn't quite taken responsibility for my self-inflicted wounds. I had become so used to blaming other people for my problems that I totally avoided what part I played in my pain and suffering. There was a lot of work ahead to finally heal the wounds that were covered with Band-Aids for thirty years.

Once Jayllen was off to school the next morning, I decided to give my homework a shot. I sat down in from of a full length mirror in my bedroom just staring at my reflection for about two minutes. I opened my mouth slowly and started to whisper my reasons as if I was trying to keep someone else from hearing. My reasons had names, names of all the boys and men I shared my temple with. I was hurt, I was broken and my soul was fragmented. No matter where those guys were in the world there was a piece of me with them. I was the literal definition of "all over the place" but I knew that I was fixable. I declared healing over my life, and took it a step further. I grabbed my cell phone out of my purse and sent text messages to every one of the guys whose number was saved in my contacts. *"Hey I just wanted to apologize for granting you permission to take advantage of the vulnerable insecure soul that I once was. While forgiving me, I have chosen to forgive you as well. You don't have to respond to this text message; I am doing this for me. I wish you all the best. −Ebony"* I closed and locked the doors that I opened when I gave them permission to mistreat me.

Sometimes we have to forgive other people even if we never receive the "I'm sorry" that we think we deserve. I took matters into my own hands in taking my power back. I proceeded to write a letter to each of my parents. I had no intentions on sharing the letters with my parents. I simply used them to express my feelings uninterrupted. I gave myself permission to feel every ounce of abandonment, resentment and hatred that I felt for my parents one LAST time. I experienced every emotion imaginable. I cried, I screamed, in the end I forgave myself for believing for then thirty years that it was my fault that my parents didn't care for me. I spoke aloud that I forgave my mother and father and fell asleep that evening light hearted.

I couldn't wait to get to back Jeremy's office for our next session to disclose all the progress I made. Pastor Sim was right. Counseling was not correction it was direction. I felt free to just be each time I sat on the brown couch in Jeremy's office. It was a judgement free zone. He seemed so elated when I returned with the great news of all the inner work I'd done. He jokingly expressed that I didn't need him anymore. He was curious to know had I spoken with DeVonn, I told him I hadn't. I wasn't ready yet. He suggested that I learned to *kill* DeVonn with kindness. So I did, anytime from that day forward if I disagreed with him, I kept it to myself. If I had to get off the phone to kick, scream or cry I did it in private. I never allowed him to see or hear me respond to his actions ever again. Gentle Reminder: "He, who angers you, controls you." I even reached the point of responding to his discouraging e-mails with compliments from Jayllen's teachers or information on Jayllen's academic success.

It was my way of letting him know that our son's growth and

development meant more to me than any e-mail he could send. My attention was now geared towards becoming a whole woman so that I could raise a whole, well rounded child. I had to be mentally well to do so. I was no longer sharing control of my thoughts and mind with anyone. Since then we have become the best co-parents and it has continued for years now. The reason why is because we have had many restorative conversations, which has given us an opportunity to forgive one another for what was, and realized that nothing else matters, but Jayllen. **#KidsLivesMatter** We play two different positions but we are on the same team with one dream to see our son become the best version of himself. We are really patient with each other and fight hard to understand the other even when we don't always agree.

I only had four sessions with Jeremy before I started receiving several phone calls from unknown phone numbers on October 7th, 2014. I was sending all of the unknown callers to voicemail right before my grandmother called. I answered thinking I must be missing something important.

"Hello."

"Hey baby."

"Hey grandma is everything good."

"I just got off the phone with your Aunt Lola, your grandma passed away today."

"My grandma didn't pass away; I'm on the phone with my grandma."

"Your daddy's mother, sweetheart."

"Oh, I'm sorry to hear that, I don't mean any disrespect but I didn't know her."

"You should call and check on your daddy."

"Why? The last time I talked to him he told me he wasn't my daddy, I have moved on with life."

"Ok baby, it's up to you."

The forgiveness I'd claimed to grace my dad with weeks prior was tested early. I wasn't going to call him though. I must have received phone calls from twenty different people over the next few days. Everybody was begging me to go check on my daddy. I was curious to know how did everybody get my phone number all of a sudden and how many of them called him in the last thirty years to say please go check on Ebony? After my grandma asked me to go a second time, I decided I would but not without someone I knew. I called one of my cousins from his side of the family to ask her will she go over to the house with me. She told me that she had just left the house but if I could get there in ten minutes she would turn around and meet me there so that I wasn't alone and uncomfortable.

I followed the driving instructions given to me by my cousin and drove slowly to my paternal grandmother's home. I pulled up and it looked like a family reunion, I didn't know anyone. As soon as I got out of the car, my daddy stood up and walked to the car to greet us. He hugged me and said "I'm so glad you came to see about me, who this big fella with you" I said this is my son Jayllen. He smiled and hugged Jayllen as he looked up at me to say, "This is my only grandson." He escorted us to the porch where everybody was sitting and looking at me like Exhibit A at a local elementary school science fair. Before I sat down I asked him where his deranged wife was. I'd never seen her before I didn't want to be caught off guard. He told me she wasn't there, and that she doesn't leave home often. He introduced me to everybody. His siblings were the only people that knew of my existence. I had first cousins my age that I was so glad I hadn't run into and gotten myself involved with.

It is very challenging to make me uncomfortable. I am a peoples person, the girl that will have you sitting in your car wondering how you just engaged in a thirty minute conversation with a stranger in Walmart on aisle three by the peanut butter. However, there I was that day with thirty years' worth of questions built up inside of me and I couldn't formulate a sentence if my life depended on it. I excused myself from the porch to make a run to the store to buy a twelve pack of Lima-A-Ritas and a six pack of bud light, so that I could relax and hopefully engage in conversation. When I returned I offered my dad a Bud Light only to find out he had been sober for ten years. He was speaking a foreign language, people actually functioning without alcohol was news to me. After I consumed a few lime-a-ritas I had a little liquid courage, I started answering and asking all types of questions. I asked him, "what was his mother like, what was her name what did she look like?" he reached under his chair for a photo album; opened the album directly to baby photos of me. My eyes got big and watery. My heart smiled. I meant something to somebody for them to put my pictures in a photo album. What really broke me that evening was when my cousins started to question me with ever answer I gave I heard my dad's voice mumbling the same answers. He knew more about me than I could have ever imagined.

When I was heading inside to use the restroom, he asked me could he hold my car keys so that he could move my car out of the road. I was inebriated, struggling to make sense of anything so I gave him my keys. I never made it back outside to see where he actually moved my car. It wasn't until later that evening when I was saying my goodbyes that he told me he moved my car inside the gate because he didn't want me driving under the influence. Jayllen and I slept on the couch that night, while he slept on the recliner. Every time I made the slightest move he would wake up to ask me was I ok. It was almost as if I was a helpless newborn baby in his eyes.

I didn't know that my daddy was the oldest of his siblings and that the entire family seemed to depend on him for everything. He was carrying his whole family on his shoulders. He was like the strong friend that is always there for everybody but the friend that nobody ever calls to check on. That troubled me a little bit. I had to restrain myself from jumping into their family business. I was extremely cautious about getting attached too quickly. I didn't know how long our budding relationship would last and I didn't want to set myself up for any more disappointment. I never thought it was possible to miss something that you never had until I started spending time with my daddy. I went to visit him at the house every day leading up to the funeral. He asked me would I be able to make it to the funeral because he really needed me there. I told him I wasn't sure because I had to work.

The day of the funeral one of his good friends called and begged me to come; I told him I couldn't make any promises. My heart wouldn't allow me stay at work that day, I understood then that forgiveness just like love is an action word as well. I'd truly forgiven my father. I told my supervisor that I was taking an early lunch so I could go console my daddy. When I arrived to the church I walked to the bathroom so that when I walked back out I could make eye contact with him, when he saw me he smiled and I smiled back and went to find a seat. I sat near my first cousins and I saw their tears and heard their cries, I could only imagine the hurt from losing a grandmother because I was raised by one. I just wish I knew the joy of having a relationship with my grandmother that was in the casket.

I went back to work after the funeral with a full heart. I knew I did the right thing. Jayllen and I went back to the house when I got off from work, only to find out that his wife caught wind that I was visiting him and I was at the funeral earlier that day. I told him I was going to leave before she came over there to start a confrontation. He said she's not coming anywhere, she doesn't drive. I said you mean to tell me all these years that she's been threatening me she was going to need someone to bring her to me to actually see her threats through. He said, yep. We both laughed. We finally got a chance to talk that evening after the house cleared out and everyone was gone home. He said, "Ebony, you have the right to feel any way you choose towards me, I deserve it." I told him that I had already forgiven him. He said "God took my mother away from me, but the only reason I am at peace is because He gave me my daughter back."

When I went to see my daddy the first day, I felt like other people forced me to do it and I wanted to back him in the corner with telling him how much he ruined my life. I knew within minutes of being around him that he had beaten himself down enough in thirty years; he didn't deserve my beating too. I went back the second and third day, and to the wake and funeral because I wanted to know what happens after forgiveness. Restoration! It wasn't God's plan for me to have a relationship with my paternal grandmother, because it would be her death that He used to restore the relationship between my father and I. When I became good enough for my daddy, I became good enough for me. When God told me to end my last relationship back in the beginning of 2014, I had no idea it was because my fatherless void would finally be filled with my actual father by the end of 2014. My days of searching for random men to fill in the blanks had come to an end. I'd finally found the right **answer**.

My dad and I speak very often now. He loves me but he is *crazy* about his only grandson. We have a relationship that only God could have mended back together. Not only have I forgiven my father, but I have also offered him a clean slate. We've all made mistakes in our past, what good is forgiving if we're not going to forget. We can't hold other people to their past and ask God to do a new thing in us at the same time. We have to be willing to forgive just as fast as we want to be forgiven.

12

NEW BEGINNING

Ebony K. English

Two days before New Year's Eve 2014, my daddy called to ask me what church was I going to attend. I told him I hadn't made plans to attend church at all. He suggested that we go to my mother's church. I was apprehensive about it because I didn't know how my mom would feel about seeing my dad nor did I know how her boyfriend would respond. I called to ask her if she thought it would be a good idea. To my surprise she didn't have any objections. Two days later I was sitting in church with my mother on my left and my daddy on my right. I was nestled in the middle like a five year old little girl with the feelings to match. In real time I was thirty years old and in the same room with both of my parents for the first time. My dad had a plan when he asked me to go to my mother's church that evening. He hoped that I would give my mother the same grace of forgiveness I had given him. I did. Ironically, the name of my mother's church is New Beginning. God needed me to forgive my parents before He could offer us just that, a new beginning. As long as I was entitled with the mindset that my parents owed me something, I was blocking my own blessings. Would I have liked a more storybook type of love from my parents? Abso-freaking-lutely, but my willingness to grow and forgive allowed God to soften my heart as He showed me that my parents loved me the best way that they knew how. Because 2014 was the year that I made peace with my pieces, 2015 was the year God used those same pieces to put me back together again.

We were a little over three weeks into the year 2015 when I went to support one of my friends at a concert. I didn't know that would be the night I had my last *dance* with, "Jose Cuervo" (tequila). The next morning I woke up to Jayllen standing beside my bed crying and asking was I sick the night before, I said, "no baby why" as I stepped out of bed into my own vomit. I was so ashamed. I've had many hangovers, some so embarrassing that I had to call someone to bring Jayllen something to eat because I couldn't move out of bed. That didn't compare to me having to apologize to my son for scaring him. I knew when I looked into his eyes that I had to make a different decision.

Wrecking my car didn't change my behavior, seeing the tears in my grandmother's eyes as she begged me on several occasions not to drink and drive didn't change my behaviors, putting my life in danger every time I got behind the wheel or under a man while being intoxicated wasn't enough for me to stop drinking. God knew it would take Jayllen for me to wake up and pay attention. I was deathly afraid to fail at parenting and I believe what doesn't heal gets passed down to our children. If I wasn't strong enough to carry my burdens, I knew my then seven year-old son didn't have the muscle to carry it either. I told God in the moment of standing right next to my vomit, "I don't know if it's possible, but I am willing to try." I never labeled my dysfunction, but I was all too familiar with the lifestyle. The first order of business, if I was going to defeat the beast I had to call it out by its name. Alcoholism, and I was a functioning alcoholic.

I had no idea what the non-drinking process would look or feel like, but I did know I didn't want my son's childhood memories to consist of having an alcoholic for a mother. Snatching me off the road of self-sabotage and guiding me down the road of sobriety was a job for Jesus. My job was to trust the process and follow His lead. On January 23rd, 2015 I set out on a journey to live a sober life. Every morning when I woke up in the days following I would look in the mirror and tell myself how pretty and worthy I was sober. The little girl inside of me needed to hear that, so the grown Ebony looking back at me in the mirror could flourish into everything God created her to DO and BE!

When I started to tell people that I don't drink anymore I would receive responses like, "we've heard that before," "we'll see how long it last this time." Nobody believed it was possible not even me, but the train was moving and every day I was picking up speed. As the weeks passed I would receive phone calls from family and friends asking so you still not drinking. "No, I don't drink anymore," I would reply. The phone calls came less and less and people that I would see on a regular basis started to disappear. That was the most hurtful part about my journey. When I was dying on the inside I was surrounded by people, but when I was starting to get a little pep in my step, walking in the direction of who I was created to be, the faces around me were few.

Sometimes what seems like people turning their back on us is God isolating us. I was a co-depending approval addict for as long as I could remember. Isolation is how God got my undivided attention. He desired an intimate relationship with me; He drew me closer to Him through my loneliness.

One day while starting to miss my adult interactions the holy spirit led me to 1 Peter 4: 2-4 which reads: *you won't spend the rest of your lives chasing your own desires, but you will be anxious to do the will of God. You have had enough in the past of the evil things that godless people enjoy-their immorality and lust, their feasting and drunkenness and wild parties, and their terrible worship of idols. Of course your former friends are surprised when you no longer plunge into the flood of wild and destructive things they do. So they slander you.* I relied heavily on that scripture when loneliness tried to creep in and distract me in my season of transitioning from a substance abuser to a woman of substance.

ဆၣ

Sobriety wasn't a one-time decision. It is a choice that I have to make every 24 hour period.

Sobriety wasn't a one-time decision. It is a choice that I have to make every 24 hour period. My sobriety is now a top priority of mine. I do whatever is necessary to protect it. However, I don't want to glamorize sobriety so much that it becomes misleading. I have had moments of struggle when I left out of the house just to go to the store so that I could rub my fingers across wine bottles, or when I would ask people to just let me smell it. But then I remember all the things that alcohol stole from me that God was restoring through sobriety and it just isn't worth it. Most importantly I remember that my son has been watching me relentlessly move from the pits to promise and from hangovers to healing. I will not give alcohol control over our lives again.

During some of my earlier days in sobriety while trying to navigate through the path of "what now", I had some very unsure moments full of self-doubt. Thankfully, not having alcohol to drown out my thoughts I was able to feel and address those feelings. One of the major things I discovered is that aside from battling with a mind altering substance; I was also operating with a life altering set of limiting beliefs that were hindering my growth as well. There was a pre-recorded programming that was controlling my life. I chose to no longer follow that program and focused on the reprogramming and development of a new set of beliefs about who I was becoming. I trained my subconscious mind to believe in my sobriety, just as I had trained it to believe that I needed alcohol to function.

ഇരുന്

Being sober wasn't my goal. Gaining hope, dreaming again, living my best life and falling madly in love with myself was the ultimate goal.

Sobriety has allowed me to think clearer thoughts and heal in a way I could have never dreamed possible. Remember when I told you all that there was a part of me that didn't want to be rescued? That is because I was afraid to heal. Healing from the inside out forced me to come face to face with "why." "Why" is a big bad three letter word that leaves us naked and exposed with little room to blame other people for our lack of becoming who God created us to be. It's easy to forfeit our healing because we don't want to be held accountable for the part that we played in our own heartache, pain, and self-destruction. But what if I told you that your breakthrough is on the other side of you standing in your "naked truth" and your willingness to finally answer the "why" you've been avoiding? Why do I drink so much? Why do I need to be validated? Why do I allow myself to remain in toxic relationships? Why do I attract the type of men that I do? "Why do I believe in others more than I believe in myself? These are just a few of the "why" questions I had to answer to unlock my healing. Your list may look a little different, but your healing is depending on you to conquer that big bad three letter word. You don't have to exploit yourself in front of the world. But why not expose your heart and your true intentions to yourself so you can cancel the subscription of negative chatter going on between your ears and finally open up your heart to what God has been saying about you all along.

As a woman it comes natural to pick up everybody else's "stuff", leaving our "stuff" to linger and go wherever the wind blows. I want to challenge you to go get your "stuff" back that the enemy has stolen from you. You're not too scattered that God can't make you whole again, but He needs you to bring Him the pieces. Being sober wasn't my goal. Gaining hope, dreaming again, living my best life and falling madly in love with myself was the ultimate goal. Sobriety was the name of the ship that it all sailed in on. Your ship may have a different name on it but you owe yourself another shot at sailing. I declare and decree that your *sinking days* are now a thing of the past.

Ebony K. English

13

UNAPOLOGETIC

I was snuggled in bed all day the day after Thanksgiving 2016 craving barbecue chicken nachos from Wild Wings and waiting for DeVonn to pick Jayllen up for the weekend. He arrived at our apartment around 7:15 that evening and I was in Wild Wings parking lot at exactly 7:33pm when my phone rang. I looked down to see it was Aunt Mini calling. I sent her to voicemail, I was too hungry to hold a conversation. She called right back which usually indicated an emergency, so I answered.

Me: "Yoooo."

Her: "What you doing girl?"

Me: "I'm walking in Wild Wings finally coming to get these nachos I've been thinking about all day."

Her: "Oh, who is with you?"

Me: "I'm by myself, anymore questions?"

Her: "Seriously, who are you with?"

Me: "Aunt Mini, man I'm by myself."

Her: "Oh, somebody killed Johnny."

Me: "What Johnny, big Johnny?"

Her: "No Eb, Lil Johnny."

I let off a scream that could be heard across the entire Harbison Blvd as my body instantly fell too numb for me to feel it hit the ground in Wild Wings parking lot. Something was lost in translation. There was no way Johnny had transitioned. I peeled myself up off the ground and called my aunt back to ask her what was I supposed to do. She told me to come to his house. She answered with instructions with what to do in that moment. I needed to know what I was supposed to do with my life. I have never known life without my Johnny and Matt. We are first cousins, born to three sisters in the same year. It had always been the three of us. Those are my *brothers* and to hear the news that we were tragically reduced to two at the age of thirty-two years old was unfathomable.

I drove to his house with a knot in my throat and not knowing what to expect, but hoping it was a cruel, I mean really cruel joke. The closer I got to his house, the more cars I saw in the yard. I felt my pulse beginning to race. I turned my headlights off so that I could pull up close to the front porch as I attempted to slow my breathing down. As soon as I walked through the door, the first person I saw was Matt. Our eyes met and the slow nodding of his head up and down and the lack of words spoken between us diminished any doubt that it could possibly be a lie. I turned back around to sit in my car for a few minutes. I needed to feel the reality of what was or I knew I would sabotage my sobriety to numb the reality of what was. I had no desire to be hugged on and told that everything will be ok. I knew eventually it would be, but that night it was everything except okay. When Matt and I did get close enough to each other again to where we could exchange words, the first thing he said was, "it's just us, cousin," I shook my head. I wasn't ready to accept it yet. I spent the whole weekend in disbelief and keeping a close eye on Matt. We were all inseparable, but their bond was a tad bit different because they're males, they had done and said things together that I had no idea about neither would I understand.

The recent turn of events put me in a tough predicament. I was accepted into a Recovery Coach training program that week which would require me to be out of town the full week after Johnny passed away. I was torn between do I stay with my family or do I push through to obtain a certification that would catapult my life to the next level. I trusted myself to make the right decision, but was still concerned about how it would be received by family if I decided to participate in the program. I solicited the opinion of two people Matt (who invested in the program on my behalf) and my friend Troy. Matt said, "Cousin, it's hard but we still have to live after this, I think you should go." Troy suggested, "Stay with your family, you all need each other right now." Knowing that I would never forgive me for giving up on myself again or leaving my family, I took the advice of both. I decided I would drive to training in the mornings and drive back home to be with my family in the evenings. Sometimes we have to be uncomfortable to acquire the desires of our heart. Driving back and forth that week also put me in position to play a game of catch me if you can with the repo man as my car was definitely on the chopping block.

I spent the majority of my week in a classroom with recovering drug addicts and alcoholics and on breaks I was trusted with the task of writing and compiling photos for Johnny's obituary. I was not only given the opportunity to learn more about addiction, I was also gifted the opportunity to view life through two different lenses. Through one lens, I saw thirteen addicts who have experienced the pits of their life and been redeemed with a chance to do a new thing, an opportunity to make some new decisions. Through the other lens, I saw my cousin who had also seen the pits of his life, but his opportunity to do a new thing had expired. The reality that God had placed me in position to witness that week is we just don't have the time that we think we do.

On Friday December 2nd, 2016 I received my Recovery Coach certification two hours before I rushed back down the road to attend Johnny's funeral and burial services. I excused myself from the repass. I didn't have an appetite for food that day, I had an appetite to maximize the potential of every dream I let die, every part of my story I was ashamed of, and purpose that I was running from. When we gathered back at his house that evening, I heard the voices of my family saying, "Eb, you not even going to take one shot for Johnny?" I heard the small voice in my head saying, "You can smoke some weed, to cope with your feelings. That wasn't your substance of choice." I also heard some of the last words my cousin said to me, "Girl, I heard you don't drink anymore. I am so proud of you." Taking a shot would have been too easy. Succumbing to the mind altering effects of marijuana would have been easy as well. I decided the only way for me to honor Johnny's life is to start living mine, UNAPOLOGETICALLY. While I still have time.

ഇ)ൠ

I decided the only way for me to honor Johnny's life is to start living mine, Unapologetically. While I still have time.

Ebony K. English

FINAL THOUGHTS

Who I am, is NOT who I have always been, by the grace of God I've not only survived, but I'm thriving!! Through all the disappointment, rejection and pain my purpose has been revealed. I thank all who have contributed to my story. You all don't owe me a single thing, in fact I OWE YOU! Without you I simply would not be who I am! There isn't a soul that has flipped through these pages that I don't have love for. I think the world of all of you and as a reminder that same world is yours for the taking so be sure to let the enemy know that you're coming to get your hope, your healing and your breakthrough.

In closing, I'll leave you all with this, *"It's ok if you fall down and lose your spark. Just make sure that when you get back up you rise as the whole damn fire!"*-unknown

Sending you loads of love and more hugs than you can handle!
-*El*

ABOUT THE AUTHOR

Ebony K. English is a mother, influencer, speaker, and author. A Class of 2002 graduate of Columbia High School, a proud Benedict College Tiger, and a true southern girl born and raised in Columbia, South Carolina.

Growing up in Columbia, South Carolina Ebony struggled to find her place in the crowd, and always felt like the underdog. At a very young age she battled with insecurities, anger, resentment and a broken heart due to the absence of her biological father. In attempt to fill her fatherless void, she often found herself suffering in silence and using alcohol as a coping mechanism. After 12 years of alcohol dependency she was delivered from alcoholism in January of 2015 and has since transferred all dependency to God; our one true healer.

Turning pain into purpose, she is now a voice for silent sufferers, a Certified Recovery Coach, a Peer Support Specialist to homeless adolescents in her community, and Founder of Saved, Sober & Sitting Pretty an organization that inspires women to live their lives on purpose and declare victory over the battle of alcoholism and other addictions.

ಬಾCಿR

www.ebonykenglish.com

FB: Ebony K. English

IG: @ebonykenglish

ebonykenglish@gmail.com

Ebony is a 2017 South Carolina Black Pages Top 20 under 40 honoree that is an encouraging force to all she encounters. Finding peace with her pieces has motivated her to share her story to all open hearts and ears as she speaks to the conqueror inside all of us. She is very passionate about meeting women where they are; loving them enough to get where they are going and celebrating them on their journey as they transition from substance abuse to Women of Substance. Using the power of transparency, speaking from the heart, sharing very emotional stories of triumph, and loving on people who are where she once was is a gift that she proudly possesses. Her impactful message encourages the young and the young at heart to acknowledge their power, passion, purpose and to show up for their own lives, use their voices to speak loudly, and to max out in reaching their full potential!

Ebony K. English

.

www.ingramcontent.com/pod-product-compliance
Lightning Source LLC
Chambersburg PA
CBHW072155090426
42740CB00012B/2277